PAUL McCartney
BASSMASTER

PAUL
McCartney
BASSMASTER

playing the great
beatles basslines

Paul McCartney with the Beatles at Wembley Studios in
London during rehearsals for a 1964 US TV special

PAUL MCCARTNEY: BASSMASTER
PLAYING THE GREAT BEATLES BASSLINES

by Tony Bacon & Gareth Morgan

A BACKBEAT BOOK
First edition 2006
Published by Backbeat Books
An Imprint of Hal Leonard Corporation
7777 West Bluemound Road,
Milwaukee, WI 53213
www.backbeatbooks.com

Devised and published for Backbeat Books by
Outline Press Ltd,
2A Union Court, 20-22 Union Road,
London SW4 6JP, England.
www.jawbonepress.com

ISBN: 978-0-87930-884-1

A catalogue record for this book is available from the British Library.

EDITOR: Ian James
DESIGN: Paul Cooper Design

Printed by Regent Publishing Services Limited, China

12 13 14 15 16 6 5 4 3 2

contents

McCartney in his element: on stage with bass in hand

something in the way he played

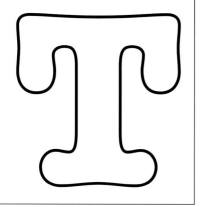

here is no greater compliment than respect from your peers for your craft, skill, musicianship, and musicality. "He's the guvnor,"[i] says Sting, simply and appropriately. "Paul McCartney always comes to mind first as a major influence, for the melodic and musical way he approaches his parts," says Mike Elizondo of Dr Dre.[ii] There are any number of similar accolades from past and present bass players.

But what really elevates Paul McCartney is the fact that your average Joe on the street is likely to say: "Oh yeah, he played that tiny violin thing. He was good, wasn't he?" That kind of acknowledgement eclipses even the weightiest tome written by any respected, pre-eminent musicians or academics. That kind of praise, after all, comes from the real world.

Anybody who truly innovates will be much copied. Musicians are like a flock of sheep. No disrespect intended, just a simple acknowledgement that 'lifting' or 'copying' or 'copping' are legitimate ways to learn or expand what we do. And there are plenty of players who have based the main body of their playing on what McCartney played and how he played it with The Beatles.

Listen carefully and you'll hear recognisable McCartney-isms seeping from the grooves of any number of guitar-based pop bands right up to the present day – and you should expect to be able to survey pop music 20 years from now and still find this to be the case, such is his impact. XTC's Colin Moulding describes his own fine playing as "the bastard son of [Free's] Andy Fraser and Paul McCartney".[iii] We'd argue that Fraser himself was strongly influenced by McCartney, too. Think about it: the tight, growling, yet rubbery tone that leaked from Fraser's short-scale Gibson EB-3 bass, and that solid-quarter-notes-with-a-twist chorus part alongside the

gorgeous interval-leap bassline under Paul Kossoff's classic guitar solo in 'Alright Now'. Can you think of anyone else who might have made similar choices in such a situation? Exactly.

But nobody realises those ideas as effectively or makes them sound so naturally played, so effortless and in control, as McCartney. If you're gonna steal 'em, as Marcus Miller would say, you gotta flip 'em. And if you don't? Then your playing, compared to the originator, will sound like it hasn't caught sight of the sun for a very long time.

With every great bass player, everything knits together into a unique blend, including their sound, feel, range, and the melodic or rhythmic appeal of their ideas. McCartney wins his membership to the club of greatness because, just like Victor Bailey or Stanley Clarke, you can't help but instantly recognise him when you hear his sound on record. Remember, what you play does not have to be technically difficult to be innovative and influential – and many of McCartney's best lines have the 'wow' factor because of their sheer beauty as independent melodies or the almost poetic way that they pull the whole song together. Not that McCartney fails to deliver serious chops when he feels like it, whether it be the full three minutes of classics such as 'Rain' or simply a tasty morsel of a fill here and there.

A top bass player must be a trendsetter, too. Larry Graham and Stanley Clarke showed us how to use our thumbs and Jaco Pastorius opened our eyes to the possibilities and beauty of fretless bass. Francis Rocco Prestia proved that you can fill the whole bar with sixteenth-notes at a wide range of tempos and still groove deep in the pocket. Of the contemporary greats, Victor Wooten pushes the envelope so often that you begin to think he could do anything on a bass that he set his mind to – and all with a broad grin.

McCartney's basslines educated a different sort of listening public and musician. The Beatles were so popular that any chances he took on bass were immediately and microscopically scrutinised, far more than any of his contemporaries, including John Entwistle and Jack Bruce. Such was the focus on The Beatles' every breath that the stakes became unfeasibly high. Many with less faith and belief in their own ability would have become creatively constipated under such pressure, but McCartney blossomed. There was a real sense of adventure and exuberance in many of McCartney's lines from *Rubber Soul* onwards, and this helped to clear away forever the stagnant atmosphere around many pop-group rhythm sections.

You want the bassline on a song to be the second most dominant voice after the main (vocal) melody? Well, McCartney did it and the records sold in millions. You want to play expansively and funkily for the full three minutes? That's OK: McCartney did that in 'Taxman'. The number of Beatles songs whose pace and direction are set by McCartney's bassline are numerous and varied. He was the first bass-playing captain and navigator of the good ship Pop Song and his playing with The Beatles are works of pure, instinctive genius. While we need to steer clear of anything as wholly unreasonable and dangerous as deification, we can justifiably use terms like genius and inspired. Influential musicians are, after all, only human.

By the time McCartney was really blossoming on *Revolver* he had already displayed another of the qualities that marks out the great bassman: a musical instinct that led him to make the right choices. He was never afraid of hard work. Beatle folklore has him as usually the last one to leave the session, the one who did the most work on any of the songs, and the one who was the most interested in a high level of excellence in writing, performing, and recording. It is this that gave many people – including members of The Beatles themselves – the impression that it had become a one-man show by the time *Let It Be* hit the stores, and that this, alongside reputed friction between peripheral 'members' of the band, caused the group to split up. In truth, the demise of the Beatles was probably triggered by the death of Brian Epstein in 1967 and accelerated by the ill-advised establishment of Apple. It was the ensuing business nightmares that finally drove a wedge between the three major creative members of the group.

All of this should not be bound up with the way The Beatles made music

(and, in practice, it never really was) or the way that McCartney functioned in general or specifically on bass. The desire and willingness to work hard was an ethic instilled in McCartney from a very early age. He was never exactly on the breadline, but he didn't live in suburban luxury either, and being prepared to put in the hours should never count against anyone. We're not claiming that he woodshedded in his bedroom for months on end to hone his chops.

He spent many, many hours playing and thinking about bass guitar. Go back and try to calculate the proportion of their working life that the group spent in the studio simply developing songs, working out parts, doing takes, overdubbing, re-working pieces, and generally honing their material before it was released – and all among a punishing touring schedule that continued to late 1966. This was better than any repetitive scale practice or the continual refinement of licks with a drum machine. Nobody ever worked harder on their music prior to The Beatles and precious few have worked so hard since.

McCartney made it cool to be a bass player, especially as he was the first to co-front a band with only four strings under his fingers. There is a common preconception – one that, sadly, still holds some water to this day – that the singer and then the guitar player were the hip ones, the ones who attracted the most attention from the opposite (or same) sex. McCartney made it OK for bass players to actually crave the spotlight and to manipulate it for whatever end they chose. Forget the bloke-next-door all-round-entertainer persona he chose to wear post-Beatles. When he was the bass player in the Fab Four, Paul McCartney was seriously good. This book, we hope, will show you precisely why.

TONY BACON & GARETH MORGAN
somewhere in England, May 2006

Beatle bassist in waiting – with Stu Sutcliffe already out of focus

early years

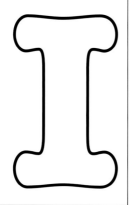n the space of two weeks in April 1966, Paul McCartney played some of the best bass guitar of his life. It began with 'Paperback Writer' on Wednesday 13th, continued during the next few days with 'Rain', then 'Taxman' the following Thursday, 'And Your Bird Can Sing' on Tuesday 26th, and 'I'm Only Sleeping' the day after that. Each is a little masterpiece where McCartney takes the four-string electric bass to a level that neither he nor any other player had achieved before. The Beatles' bassman was almost at the height of his powers. He was taking risks and experimenting with sounds, and both elements came together in a wonderfully appropriate tone.

"The beautiful innocence you had, that was the thing about it," says McCartney. "We were just discovering it all, making it up as we went along, and there wasn't an awful lot of time to think about it – which I think is always a good thing. The more time you've got to think about it, the more time you've got to worry. I kind of like just trusting your instincts, where you're on … holy shit! Then you're off."[1]

Since the time the group had started earlier in the decade, McCartney's bass playing became more and more important to the melodic and harmonic development of their songs. His thoughtful and often unconventional approach did a great deal to liberate the bass from its accustomed role. In the early 1960s most bass players simply provided unexciting and unchallenging root notes under the chord progression. McCartney was coming up with ever more interesting and inventive basslines, pushed further and further forward in the mix as The Beatles' recordings became as revolutionary as their composing skills.

How did McCartney get there? He'd started out as a guitarist in John Lennon's group, which became The Beatles. Before that, his dad had bought him a trumpet. "But I realised I couldn't sing with the trumpet," he remembers, "and I wanted to sing as well. So I asked [my dad] if he wouldn't mind if I traded it in for a guitar."[2]

The young McCartney picked up a cheap acoustic and started to learn to play guitar. But soon it became obvious that something was wrong: the guitar was right-handed; he was left-handed. "I didn't know what you did about that, there were no

rule books," he recalls. "Nobody talked about being left-handed. So I tried it right-handed and I couldn't get any rhythm, because it was all the wrong hand doing it." Then he saw a picture of left-handed balladeer Slim Whitman in a music paper and noticed the guitar pointing the 'wrong' way. "So I thought that's good, you *can* have it the other way round. Then I changed the strings around."

Left-handed guitar players do have an advantage over their right-handed colleagues, to balance any difficulties they might encounter in finding a suitable instrument. Most left-handed people are forced quite early on in their lives to do some things with their right hand, and so quickly get used to the benefits of a degree of ambidexterity. The result is that a left-handed guitarist will almost always have, potentially, a better balance of mobility between fretting and picking hand than right-handers.

Back to those early years, and the young McCartney met John Lennon and George Harrison. "George used to get on the same bus," he says. "We got chatting and he had an interest in guitars and music like I did, and we kind of hung out and became good friends. Meanwhile I'd met John through another friend of mine, and he'd asked me to join The Quarrymen, which was the very first group. I kind of went in first of all as lead guitarist, really, because I wasn't bad on guitar. And when I wasn't on stage I was even better. But when I got up on stage my fingers all went very stiff and then found themselves underneath the strings instead of on top of them. So I vowed that night that that was the end of my career as the lead guitar player. I just thought: I'll lean back."

He remembers buying a new guitar – a Rosetti Solid Seven electric – in Liverpool before the group's first trip to Germany to play in a Hamburg club. "It was a terrible guitar," he laughs. "It was really just a good looking piece of wood. It had a nice paint job, but it was a disastrous, cheap guitar. It fell apart when I got to Hamburg, the sweat and the damp and the getting knocked around, falling over and stuff. So in Hamburg, with my guitar bust, I turned to the piano. Stu Sutcliffe was a friend of John Lennon's, they were at art school together, and Stu had won a painting competition. The prize was 75 quid. We said to him, that's exactly the price of a Hofner bass! He said it's supposed to be for painting materials, but we managed to persuade him over a cappuccino."[3]

Sutcliffe became The Beatles' bass player just as soon as he'd handed over that prize money at Hessy's music store in Liverpool, bagging a lovely new Hofner 500/5, a big German hollow-body electric bass guitar. Today, McCartney says that

Sutcliffe wasn't much good as a bassist – but that, crucially, he did have that bass guitar. Back in 1964, however, he told an interviewer that Sutcliffe "was a great bass man".[4] Klaus Voormann, a friend of the group (and later bassist with Lennon's Plastic Ono Band), remembered Sutcliffe as "a really good rock'n'roll bass player. Of course, he wasn't as good a musician as the others and he was not very good technically. He couldn't have played a solo and he needed to be shown note for note, but once he understood what he had to do, he could do it and he was fine".[5]

The Beatles landed another season of gruelling gigs in Hamburg in mid 1961. "Stu had said he was gonna stay in Hamburg, he'd met a girl and was going to stay there with her and paint," says McCartney. "So it was like: 'Oh-oh, we haven't got a bass player.' And everyone sort of turned round and looked at me. I was a bit lumbered with it, really; it was like: 'Well … it'd better be you, then.' I don't think you would have caught John doing it, he would have said: 'No, you're kidding, I've got a nice new Rickenbacker!' I was playing piano and didn't even have a guitar at the time, so I couldn't really say that I wanted to be a guitarist. They'd say: 'Well get a fucking guitar then, that might be a start.'"

McCartney adds: "People have said that I did a big campaign to get the prized chair of bass. And I rang up George [Harrison] about this: 'Do you remember me edging Stu out the group so I could be the bass player?' And George said: 'No, you got lumbered with bass.' I said: 'Great, that's exactly how I remember it.'"[6]

Bass players who start out on guitar and then move over to bass play differently compared to bassists who start on bass as their first instrument. Guitarists inevitably bring guitar techniques and habits to the bass, consciously or otherwise. Maybe they'll embellish a line in a certain way or think of their basslines in terms of chords, and probably use a plectrum. As we'll see, McCartney was no exception to the trend. His grounding on six-string guitar would have an effect on his bass playing – and later would also affect his attitude to the role of the guitar in The Beatles. He said in 1964: "I believe that playing an ordinary guitar first and then transferring to bass has made me a better bass player because it loosened up my fingers. Not that I'm suggesting that every bass player should learn on ordinary guitar."[7]

For now, however, there was an urgent need for him to find a bass guitar of his own. So one day in 1961, probably around May, he went shopping in Hamburg. "Eventually I found a little shop in the centre of town, and I saw this violin-shaped bass guitar in the window." This was the first of his famous 'violin' basses, a lightweight hollow-body Hofner 500/1, made in Germany. McCartney recalls

buying this first one for around £30 (then about $50). "It was a good price. My dad had a big thing against hire purchase – what they called on the never-never. He'd lost money that way, and so he was very keen that I shouldn't do that. And we were earning reasonable money."[8] McCartney got another 500/1 a few years later and stuck to this type of Hofner as his sole live-performance bass in The Beatles and his sole studio bass until 1965.

Although he was blissfully unaware of the fact when he bought the Hofner, McCartney was in effect celebrating the tenth anniversary of the arrival of the electric bass guitar. In California in 1951 Leo Fender and some colleagues had put on sale the first such instrument, the Fender Precision. Just cast your mind back to something that happened ten years ago from now. It's not that long ago, really, is it? McCartney was taking on a relatively new and untried instrument. During the 1950s, Fender was copied by other makers, including Gibson, which in 1953 launched its EB-1 bass, and it was the general shape of this that Hofner in turn copied for their 500/1. The new Beatles bassman held in his hands that most unusual of 20th-century items, an entirely new musical instrument, and one that was yet to find its role. More than anyone else, he would help find and define that role, and in the process transform popular music.

McCartney still owns a Hofner from the Beatles days and continues to use it occasionally for live dates (especially now that he's had the intonation sorted out). But what was it like when he moved over to bass in The Beatles? "Funnily enough I'd always liked bass. My dad was a musician and I remember him giving me little lessons, not actual sit-down lessons but maybe there'd be something on the radio and he'd say: 'Hear that low stuff? That's the bass.' I remember him actually pointing out what bass was, and he'd do little lessons in harmony. So when I came to The Beatles I had a little bit of musical knowledge through him – very amateur."[9]

A "little bit of musical knowledge" is about all McCartney Jr could have had for the bass. There was no tutor industry back then: no specific electric-bass tutor books, few teachers, no handy do-as-I-do videos, DVDs, or educational TV shows, and certainly no websites to cop your licks from. Everything that McCartney played came from a fertile imagination, an innately musical mind, and extensive listening to records past and present. One of the advantages of starting bass when few people fully understood its role was that if he felt like trying something, no matter how odd or unusual, there was no precedent to say he couldn't or shouldn't.

The earliest evidence of him playing bass with The Beatles comes with the recordings that the group made, still with Pete Best on drums, in Hamburg in June 1961, backing Tony Sheridan, along with two songs on their own. These were professional recordings made under the auspices of orchestra leader Bert Kaempfert and intended for commercial release on the Polydor label. (Beyond their release at the time, three were issued on the first Beatles odds-and-ends compilation, 1995's *Anthology 1*.) McCartney sounds like an almost fully formed bass player on these recordings. There is none of the later brilliance, but he already sounds like a musician pleased with his new role. He's evidently forgotten any of those initial feelings of being lumbered with the job, which must have been shortlived. He certainly knows what he's doing.

'Ain't She Sweet' has a respectable bassline and tone, but the most interesting of the Kaempfert recordings for bass playing is a Harrison-Lennon original, a Beatles instrumental named 'Cry For A Shadow'. The enthusiastic bass playing shows that McCartney was already into and enjoying bass, while the title hints loudly at a debt to The Shadows, Britain's most successful guitar group at the time. With Jet Harris on bass, they had already scored four Top 10 singles, and their second Number 1 would hit in September. Any Brit interested in bass would have lapped up some of the Shads' B-sides – Harris's melodic riffing on 'The Stranger' or the prominent walking line on 'Midnight', for example – while on 'The Frightened City' A-side the group made a feature of a series of bass breaks by Harris.

McCartney had his ears open to many other bass players at the time. "When we started out, all we wanted to do was listen to all these great records," he said.[10] Much of the early rock'n'roll he loved was played on double-bass, whether it was Willie Dixon on Chuck Berry's Chess singles or Joe B Mauldin with Buddy Holly's Crickets. McCartney was particularly impressed by Bill Black's bass intro to Elvis Presley's 1955 single 'Baby Let's Play House'. But the relatively new electric bass guitar was making its voice heard too. In Britain, as well as Jet with The Shadows there was Brian Gregg throbbing along underneath Johnny Kidd & The Pirates, while in the States bass guitar was turning up on records by Little Richard and Jerry Lee Lewis, and Guybo Smith could be heard pounding away amid Eddie Cochran's churning mix of rockabilly, country, and blues.

Cochran was a favourite of the fledgling Beatles, although they took every opportunity to hear any American records at all that they could get hold of. While British radio back then was largely closed to rock'n'roll, Liverpool – still a busy port – was a good place to hear these otherwise rare sounds as enlightened seamen

brought back glistening pearls from overseas. "Suddenly out of the blue from America you started to hear these sounds, like Elvis Presley singing 'Heartbreak Hotel'," McCartney recalled. The group eagerly lapped up whatever they could find by Fats Domino, Little Richard, The Everly Brothers, Larry Williams, The Coasters, Bo Diddley, and more.

He added: "When we finally heard 'Heartbreak Hotel' it was unlike any other music we'd ever heard, really. It had a bit of blues in it, a bit of hillbilly, a bit of folk music, but more than that, with the echo and the sounds and the excitement of the whole thing, it was completely different, [Elvis's] own thing completely. And it became all we really talked about."[11]

There was another motivation in looking for rare music. All the groups playing in and around Liverpool and Hamburg were diligently scouting for songs to cover, drawing from the same sources. So it was a significant moment when you discovered a great little obscurity such as 'Clarabella' by The Jodimars or 'The Hippy Hippy Shake' by Chan Romero, songs that might just give you the edge over the competition.

It was important to be different and to be better in what you played. It was also important to strive for the best live sound you could achieve. In an effort to improve his bass sound, McCartney got a new speaker cabinet towards the end of 1961, custom built for him by Adrian Barber, guitarist of fellow Liverpudlian group The Big Three. The Beatles bassman teamed his existing 15-watt Selmer amp to this big new cabinet that, with its 15-inch speaker, they nicknamed the 'Coffin'. "Suddenly that was a total other world," he recalled later. "That was bass as we know it now. It was like reggae bass: it was just too right there. It was great live."[12]

The group's manager, Brian Epstein, secured them their first audition with a major record label, requiring a drive to London, and there on January 1st 1962 they recorded some demos for Decca Records. The tape survives, and five of the 15 songs were officially released on *Anthology 1*. As with the Kaempfert recordings, McCartney plays competently. His parts are not pedestrian, although equally there are no signs of impending greatness. But, again, he sounds like a bass player who wants to be a bass player and is enjoying his role in the group's developing sound.

McCartney had found a definite and interesting musical role for himself – and was competitive enough to know that the bass guitar was an instrument on which he could establish himself as an important cog in the Beatles wheel. Most of all, he certainly doesn't sound like someone who's been lumbered. And his fortunes were about to take a great change for the better.

Tuned up and ready for a take

1962 - 1965

starting at
abbey road

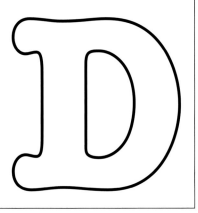

ecca famously rejected The Beatles, and they signed to Parlophone-EMI, with Ringo Starr taking over the drum stool from Pete Best. Their recording career was about to begin properly, and McCartney's bass playing would soon reach the world at large. The group's producer at Parlophone was, of course George Martin.

At the time of their first single, 'Love Me Do', first recorded in June 1962 and then remade in September, The Beatles were "quite adequate as players", said Martin. "They could play guitar pretty well and they had an uninhibited sound."[13] The single, with 'PS I Love You' on the flip, was a rarity at the time: both sides were written by members of the group. McCartney's bass playing on the recordings is safe and unsurprising. Perhaps he was nervous. (Contrast that with a version of 'Love Me Do' recorded about a year later at a radio session, released on *Live At The BBC*, which has better bass work with more ideas.)

For the second single Martin proposed a song not by Lennon & McCartney, the lightweight 'How Do You Do It'. Martin: "John sang the solo, quite well actually, but he came to me and pleaded with me. He said, 'Look, I think we can do better than this. If we write something better, can we do it?' I said yes, but you're turning down a hit. They quickly came back with 'Please Please Me', and I must confess it knocked me out. They'd worked out all the little harmonies and it was super. I said that's great, you've got your first Number 1 hit."[14]

Not only that, 'Please Please Me' is the first Beatles recording to signpost the potential in McCartney as a great bass player. It's not great in itself, but it points the way forward. What is notable is the quality of his playing and his ideas during a fine performance, effectively live in the studio. He had no right to play that throbbing eighth-note undercurrent on the verses when he should have been doing the root-fifth, root-fifth thing that any self-respecting Merseybeat bassist of the day would have played. But his instinct told him that the song needed a big kick at this point, that into the Beatle gumbo he should pour his experience of playing Chuck Berry-style machine-gun rhythm guitar parts. Whatever provoked it, the choice was a good one. As for gear, he played his Hofner 500/1 bass through a Quad II/22 amp, which he'd recently acquired to replace the ageing Selmer, and this in turn went through his big 'Coffin' speaker cabinet.

On New Year's Eve, December 1962, The Beatles were recorded live playing at the Star Club in Hamburg, their final appearance in the city where they had shaped their early sound. The recording was made on a domestic tape machine, so it's certainly not great quality. But through the mush, the bass playing again demonstrates that McCartney was by now well aware of his role as bass player. There's nothing startling in what he plays, but everything is appropriate and considered.

On 'Hippy Hippy Shake' he's playing straight eighth-notes, a technique drawn directly from his experience of rhythm-guitar playing. The song had been in their set for at least a year, so the driving rock'n'roll line might even have provided McCartney with some inspiration when he came to record 'Please Please Me'. As the revelling Beatles get to 'Ain't Nothin' Shakin' But The Leaves On The Tree' McCartney delivers a well crafted quarter-note walking line, the fast tempo apparently giving him little difficulty. Walking bass is a familiar bassist's technique, with two main elements: the first, to play a different quarter-note on each beat; the second, to imply movement. Just like going for a stroll, a walking bassline should feel like it takes you somewhere.

The Hamburg new-year tape provides the first opportunity for us to (just about) hear McCartney playing a double-stop, during 'Your Feet's Too Big'. 'Double-stop' is a term borrowed from violinists and simply means playing two notes at the same time, for colour or effect ('double' for the two notes; 'stop' as another word for fretting those notes). On the song, McCartney is working in the middle area of his Hofner's fingerboard, and he may have worried about the weaker sound this gave. A double-stop proved an effective method for him to bolster the sound – and as an ex-guitarist he would be used to root-fifth shapes from rock'n'roll six-stringing.

A well-known part of the legend now, the first Beatles album was recorded in one day at EMI's Abbey Road studios in north-west London on February 11th 1963 (although George Martin added a few keyboard overdubs days later). With the 'Please Please Me' single looking like a success, the album session was squeezed into a Monday during a break in the group's British tour, where they were playing under headliner Helen Shapiro. On Saturday they'd been performing 250 miles north, in Sunderland. They had the Sunday off to consider their repertoire, spent the Monday sweating it out in Abbey Road's Studio 2, and the following day were back up north for two gigs inside a day, in Sheffield and Oldham.

McCartney recalls the typical method at Abbey Road. "Me and John normally would just show everyone what the song was. In the early days we all knew, because it was from the stage act," he says. "We never rehearsed. It was very, very loose. But we'd been playing so much together as a club act that we just sort of knew it. It would bore us to rehearse too much. We kind of knew the songs, so we'd get quite a lot done at those sessions."[15] They certainly would.

EMI's recording equipment at Abbey Road was basic by today's studio standards but it was effective. For the early Beatles records, instrument and vocal microphones were fed through a simple mixing board in mono to a 2-track tape machine. Instruments were recorded on one track, voices on the other. Mixdown was a matter of balancing the two tracks and ensuring that the levels worked.

McCartney describes the atmosphere as very prim and proper in the first years that The Beatles recorded at Abbey Road with George Martin. Some have characterised the studio at the time as like a Ministry Of Recording. "Engineers had to wear shirts and ties, and all the maintenance men had white coats – it was very BBC," McCartney remembers. "But it wasn't such a bad thing, in fact. It was so organised, and there was no element of laidback about it. … For us it was like a job."[16]

The first Beatles album is a fascinating experience for those listening today with bass ears. It certainly starts with a bang: 'I Saw Her Standing There' is a wonderful group performance with a prominent and well recorded bassline. It sounds like McCartney was perfectly comfortable with the line – which is hardly surprising, because he'd lived with it for a while. He told an interviewer at the time that he'd stolen it. "Here's one example of a bit I pinched from someone. I used the bass riff from 'Talkin' About You' by Chuck Berry in 'I Saw Her Standing There'. I played exactly the same notes as [his bass player] did and it fitted our number perfectly. Even now, when I tell people about it, I find few of them believe me: therefore, I maintain that a bass riff hasn't got to be original.

"One thing I would say about learning an instrument is you should steal various bits and pieces from other guitarists and bassists," McCartney continued. "OK, so you know they belong to other people. So what? Does it really matter? I think this is a much better way of learning than with a tutor. I never had one myself and I think you can 'feel' music much more without one. With a tutor, you are told what to play and therefore get into a rut."[17]

Both 'I'm Talkin' About You' and 'I Saw Her Standing There' were in the group's live set (both were captured on that rough tape made at the Star Club a couple of months ago). Both songs feature virtually the same bassline (it's probably Willie Dixon on double-bass on the Chuck original) and McCartney naturally used the line when he came to record 'Standing There' for the album:

See 'I SAW HER STANDING THERE' next page

A count-in has been deliberately tagged on to this opening track of the group's debut album, a reminder to fans who'd heard them live. The spirited root-third-fifth bass pattern is a little more adventurous than the average straight 12-bar line and provides the main counter-melody. McCartney gets hold of his Hofner, whacked up through his Quad-Coffin rig, so you're in absolutely no doubt that there's a bass player here. Not only is he completely settled in his role, he certainly wants you to know about it. A BBC version recorded in October finds him even busier on the fingerboard, but the *Please Please Me* recording remains a defining statement in bass history. McCartney the bassman has arrived.

The first album had eight Lennon & McCartney originals among the 14 tracks, an unprecedented achievement in British pop. More importantly for us, it has many signposts to what would happen later in the group's bass department. There is standard fare: the regular roots-and-fifths approach of 'Misery'; the well executed walking bassline through 'A Taste Of Honey'. But even within those constraints there are already elements of invention. On 'Chains' he bases his part on the roots-and-fifths thing but creates ideas along the way, taking every opportunity to add appropriate colour. It's dawning on him that, through his bass, he has control over the way the song moves. 'Boys' should be a roots-and-fifths part too, but he opts for strict straight-eighths, and in the last 30 seconds (from 1:47) moves from supportive rooting into a familiar riff, lifting the end of a flagging piece as poor old Ringo gives it his all.

McCartney's considered choices of note lengths and his tactical use of ornamental 'grace notes' are evident all over *Please Please Me*. Listen, for example, to the way he clips the length of the second note in the bar of the verses in 'Anna':

See 'ANNA' next page

Most players would have just let the note ring, but McCartney already has an instinct for the groove and realises that clipping the note is a way of creating space and a funkier feel. He's listening to what's going on around him – particularly what the hi-hat needs here – as he begins to develop the arranger's ear that would serve

DO YOU WANT TO KNOW A SECRET

■ 'I Saw Her Standing There'

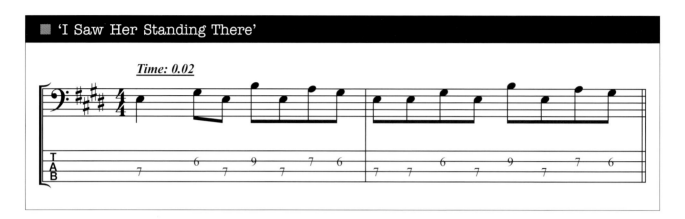

■ 'Anna'

■ 'Do You Want To Know A Secret'

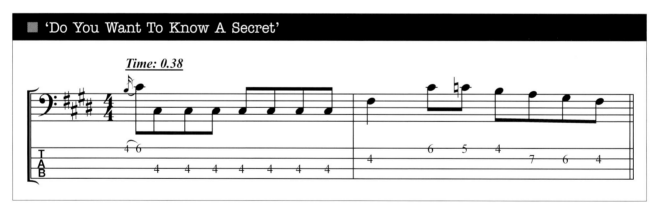

him so well in the coming years. The time that he and the group spent listening to American records was paying dividends ('Anna' itself was a Lennon favourite by black US rhythm-and-blues singer Arthur Alexander).

On 'Do You Want To Know A Secret' McCartney's bass is the second strongest voice after Harrison's vocal, a tight, well organised part with a substantial melodic content – and some mistakes. It hints generally at greater things to come. Check the verse lick from 0:38:

See 'DO YOU WANT TO KNOW A SECRET' opposite

The first album finishes with a cover of The Isley Brothers' 'Twist And Shout', a raucous belter that closed the single-day recording session. It's another good piece of playing by McCartney, but nonetheless is standard (Beatles) rock'n'roll. He'd shown he was starting to have fun with bass but implied he could do better. And he most certainly would.

They wrote and recorded their third single, 'From Me To You' / 'Thank You Girl', inside a week in March 1963, and it sounds like it. McCartney plays simply what the songs need. More interesting is that the Abbey Road engineers were now openly criticising the poor quality of his bass gear. Live, he still used his Quad-Coffin rig, but evidently it didn't please the fastidious knob-twiddlers of north-west London. "Their original sound was ... well, an absolute headache," said engineer Norman Smith. "I remember patching up their equipment – and loaning one of our amps in order to hear anything of Paul at all."[18] For this date, McCartney put his trusty Hofner through Abbey Road's loaned Leak amplifier and Tannoy speaker.

Another song recorded at the same session was 'One After 909'. The third take breaks down as McCartney fluffs his line, leading to a brief argument. "What are you doing?" asks Lennon the exasperated vocalist. "It's murder, I can't do it, can't keep it up," replies McCartney. "Get a plec!" yells someone. "I haven't got one!" the bassist shouts back, muttering about not having his cases in the studio. They'd finished the long Helen Shapiro tour just two days earlier, and the night before had played a one-off ballroom gig just outside Liverpool. The tired group manage two more incomplete takes, but the song was left unused (until released in edited form on *Anthology 1*).

The group clearly expected McCartney to use a plectrum. Was that his normal picking method? Asked recently if he used plectrum or fingers in Beatles days, he says: "I did a bit of both. Mainly, if it was a sort of important gig, I'd nearly always resort to a pick because I feel safer that way." Perhaps this was to compensate for

FINGERS OR PICK?

the bassiness of the Hofner, trying to get more treble? "Not really, no, although that is true. And with recording it helps. The engineers used to like to hear the pick because they get the treble end out as well as the bass, and then [in] the mix get it to kick right out. I used to do a little bit of both – I was never trained in any styles, so I just picked it up."[19]

On the live Beatles footage we've studied, McCartney is seen using a plectrum most of the time, 95 per cent or more, and only occasionally resorts to playing with fingers. Many other musicians who ended up on bass in the early 1960s had started out as guitar players – West Coast session player Carol Kaye is one fine example – and simply transferred their approach, with some modification, from six-string guitar to four-string bass. Many were simply offered the chance of more work by doubling on bass; some, like McCartney, slid into the role out of necessity. The little piece of plastic that he held in his left hand wasn't necessarily a big part of his tone but it did enable him and many other early bass players to be heard.

McCartney underlines the notion that they simply went for it, even in the studio. "We weren't deadly serious, not very fussy, and we used to hope that the producer didn't hear if you made a mistake. It's all so bloody righteous now, but then it was shhh," he says, finger to lips, whispering: "'If [George Martin] doesn't notice, it's all right.' And often he didn't. 'Marvellous boys, marvellous, good take.' I'm not gonna tell him if you don't, you know? It was rough and ready, but then all the early records were: that was the spirit. And they still sound good, there's a lot of spirit to them. Emerging talent!" he laughs. "Raw energy! You can hear we were going to get somewhere."[20]

Some readers have probably just thrown down the book in disgust. A mistake? Paul McCartney making a mistake? Surely not! Well, certainly. Just like all of us, he makes mistakes, even on record. One thing we ought to clear up right now is that this is a book about the real world, where great bass players are just like all other bass players in this respect: they are human beings who sometimes make mistakes. You hope the rest of the group doesn't notice and you move on.

But not before improving the gear again. Around the start of April 1963 McCartney bagged himself a new Vox T-60 transistor (solid-state) rig: a 60-watt head and a cabinet with two speakers, a 12-inch and a 15-inch. The amp would not last long; it had a nasty habit of blowing up and just about saw him through the group's UK tour supporting one of their American heroes, Roy Orbison.

Back from those dates, they dived into Abbey Road to make the fourth single,

'She Loves You' / 'I'll Get You', on July 1st 1963. The bass on the A-side is quite straightforward, but set against Ringo's playing, which works across the accents, a different feel emerges. Here McCartney allows the drummer the limelight, well aware of the importance of a group performance and his part within it. It's almost as if he calculated that with work due to start soon on the next album, he could probably save himself for that, where he'd have more space to try things out. But for the single? Keep it simple and direct. At this point in their recording career – two Top 5 singles and a Number 1 album – and as far as the music business was concerned, singles were top priority.

On the road, his Vox T-60 amp continued to play up, so before the sessions for the second album McCartney acquired a new Vox AC-30 bass head, keeping his T-60 cab. *With The Beatles* was made during July and September 1963, in something of a hurry as they grabbed time where they could between their ever-increasing whirl of activity. On that second album the recorded bass sound is often poor and ill defined, noticeably worse than the debut. The record in general sounds ragged and sloppy with obvious edits and a weak mix. It was the last Beatles album to be recorded on one of Abbey Road's old 2-track machines. On 'Little Child' McCartney might as well be playing double-bass next door given the muddy mess down below, and it's difficult to say where the bass is at all on 'Hold Me Tight'. None of this is his fault, of course, and on something like 'Not A Second Time' it's a real shame, because from the little you can hear, there seems to be some thoughtful bass stuff going on.

There are, thankfully, a few exceptions. The opener, 'It Won't Be Long', backs up the notion that McCartney was pleased to get to an album, with some extra space to try out more expansive playing. 'All I've Got To Do' is the first EMI recording to feature him playing a double-stop (two notes played together), which you can hear for the first time almost as soon as the groove comes in, at 0:04:

See 'ALL I'VE GOT TO DO' next page

'All My Loving' is a funky example of his ability to create effortless walking basslines, contrasted aptly on the chorus as he moves through the chords. And there's more evidence on 'Roll Over Beethoven' of his growing awareness that he's part of a proficient rhythm section. Listen how he cops Ringo's offbeat bass-drum and creates a not-so-obvious rhythm as a result.

It's all very well for us now with our CDs and posh amps and good speakers to criticise the sound of these early records, but how would people have heard them

A SHOT OF RHYTHM & BLUES

■ 'All I've Got To Do'

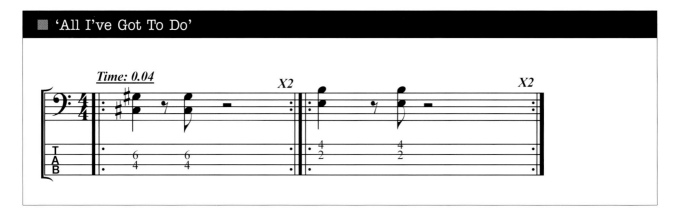

at the time? Even if there was bass-end there in the first place, it would not have been clearly audible to many listeners. When fans at the time plonked their vinyl onto a small, portable record player and let the needle drop into the groove, McCartney's bass guitar would at best have been a dull, indistinct blur in the tiny speaker.

Engineers at Abbey Road were told to limit the amount of bass-end on a record by compressing the sound when they recorded it and reducing the level as they cut the masters. They were given no choice: if there was too much bass, there was a danger that the needle would jump right out of a record's groove. It was only a little later, when engineers learned the value of bass and discerning listeners bought proper hi-fi systems to play their stereo records, that the full joy of Beatles bass became apparent.

At the BBC, engineers had no such limitations on keeping bass levels down. Perhaps they actively boosted bass, to give it more oomph on a tiny transistor radio? 'A Shot Of Rhythm And Blues', which The Beatles recorded for the BBC in August '63, certainly gives that impression, with the bass central to the performance. Maybe McCartney took a break to check out their session, broadcast on August 27th while they were playing a residency in Southport, Merseyside. If he heard it on a decent radio, he could hardly have failed to notice the effectiveness of his bass.

The group recorded plenty of BBC sessions for radio broadcasts. Playing records on air (known as 'needle time') was limited by an agreement with the Musicians' Union designed to increase work for musicians. This meant that BBC stations frequently broadcast sessions by pop groups, specially recorded more or less live at various BBC studios. Auditions were held for these sessions: The Beatles, still with Pete Best on drums, had passed theirs in February 1962, and made their first broadcast the following month, the earliest opportunity that most British pop fans outside Liverpool had to hear the group.

A large chunk of this radio material was released in 1994 on *The Beatles Live At The BBC*. Part of the attraction was the inclusion of a number of songs the group hadn't recorded elsewhere. McCartney plays well on many of the BBC takes: check out 'Young Blood' from June 1963 where he's in his stride, or 'Lucille', a treat from September where he's learned his precise singing-and-playing performance to a tee. Playing any instrument and singing at the same time, live, is a skill not to be underrated. Some, like McCartney, appear to manage it almost without effort. But it's not easy.

He got a new bass around the end of September 1963. Having played at least 170 gigs so far that year, he realised his Hofner wasn't the most hardy of instruments, so he acquired another one, keeping the old guitar as a back-up. The new Hofner 500/1 was very similar to the old 'un, but with a technical change that altered the sound. Unusually, the two pickups on the older bass were both set close to the neck, tending to give a bassier sound. The new Hofner had pickups in the conventional positions – one near the neck, one near the bridge – an arrangement that would give a slightly wider range of tones and a little better overall definition to the sound.

A new bass usually provides inspiration for any player. You pick up the new toy and, even if it's ostensibly the same as your old one, there will be differences. And it's these differences that can provoke a new twist to old lines and make your new ones even better. It can push you to fresh discoveries; it might shift your playing into a previously undiscovered gear; and it can even sharpen the mental game, simply because you're thinking 'new bass'. The new Hofner may well have altered McCartney's perception about what notes to play.

It seems to have helped in mid October when the group came to record their fifth single, 'I Want To Hold Your Hand' / 'This Boy'. They were aided by a new recording set-up, too. Abbey Road had acquired some new 4-track machines, and now The Beatles were let at one. Engineer Norman Smith explained that they would generally allocate the four tracks to "vocal; rhythm; lead; and anything else, like maracas".[21] This meant that, for now, bass and drums shared the single 'rhythm' track of Smith's scheme. Not ideal, but a listen to 'I Want To Hold Your Hand' does reveal a better bass sound compared to *With The Beatles* (although it could hardly have been worse). The new bass, with its better definition, probably encouraged McCartney to try those low-pitched double-stops (in both bridges, starting at 0:59 and 1:34). You may well cry 'accident!' but we'd argue that McCartney intended to use the technique because he wanted to add some tonal thickening. The clincher is that he can be seen miming the double-stop in this song on footage from a TV broadcast in November 1963. Yes, he really meant it. And on the record he plainly enjoys the unison part with the guitar in the main verse lick (first heard at 0:11). 'This Boy', the B-side, also reveals a clearer bass sound, and is a classy piece of playing, more expansive than you'd expect in the quasi doo-wop genre. And check that fill at 0:59:

See 'THIS BOY' below

Maybe McCartney's new bass also helped spur the group to a fine performance in Sweden when they visited late in October 1963. Or perhaps it was the prospect of all those Swedish girls. Whatever the reasons, it's worth hearing the sequence of songs played live-in-a-TV-studio and preserved on *Anthology 1*. McCartney revels in the tight tone of his new bass on the set opener, 'I Saw Her Standing There', and continues to have fun throughout. For 'You Really Got A Hold On Me' he digs into a slinky groove as he and the group appear to know effortlessly what to do. Now there's a great little band.

By the end of 1963, McCartney had made another upgrade to his Vox gear, moving to an AC-100 rig with 100-watt amp and 2x15 cabinet. It gave him all the power he needed for his new Hofner. In the new year came the now famous *Ed Sullivan* American TV-show appearances and the start of the group's startling rise in the USA. But among the growing fame there was still room for human errors. McCartney delivers a dreadfully inappropriate two-feel line to the boogie-based 'Johnny B. Goode' at a BBC session in January – but then he never thought for a moment that anyone would hear it beyond its sub-three-minute life on the airwaves.

With sessions for their third album already underway, The Beatles knocked out four tracks for an EP in March '64, largely rock'n'roll covers but with their own song, 'I Call Your Name', slipped in. Remarkably enough, the released take (seven) survived a wayward opening guitar blunder, but it's lucky for us because it allows us

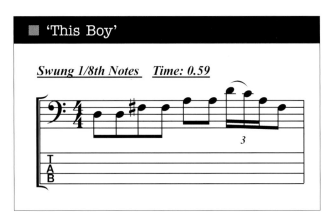

■ 'This Boy'

Swung 1/8th Notes   *Time: 0.59*

to hear a bass part still in the making. McCartney adopts a tasteful groove for the verses and some choice unison runs alongside Harrison's guitar in the choruses. Then there's an abrupt shift to a walking line under the solo (edited in from take five), barely worked out, thrillingly close to collapse at times, and hinting at some of the experimentation to come. You can almost hear him thinking: hmm, now I've got to grips with it, this bass really is a powerful musical tool. Even the old Carl Perkins song 'Matchbox' tossed to Ringo to sing for the same EP allows McCartney to trade in some serious triplet work. Check that lick at 1:47!

His growing skills had not escaped listeners with good musical ears. In a 'Player Of The Month' feature in *Beat Instrumental*, Britain's leading magazine for budding pop musicians, the writer went straight to the core. "Technically, Paul is highly rated in the beat business. There is a tendency for bass men to hover in the background, just providing a basic pounding 'thump-thump-thump' type beat to support the lead guitar and vocals. But Paul does much, much more. He puts together intricate runs which add a tremendous vibrancy and vitality to the Beatles sound."[22] Here was the earliest articulation in print of McCartney's prowess as an intelligent player – and of the rightful place for the bass in pop.

The third album, the film tie-in *A Hard Day's Night*, was recorded between February and June 1964 and is a fascinating document of the way the group in general and McCartney's bass-playing in particular were fast developing. Like all their records now, it was made on 4-track at Abbey Road. Again there is a feeling that experimentation has been reserved for the album, and there's no escaping the growing confidence and exuberance in the bass parts. It remains a subtle foreshadowing of far greater and more conspicuous things to come, but it's a welcome glimpse for all that.

Hard Day's Night is the first Beatles LP with only Lennon & McCartney songs, a unique achievement among pop groups at the time. It highlights another songwriting trend. The originally accurate 'Lennon & McCartney' credit was retained, but the two had become more likely to write individually, only occasionally with the other's help. It's well known now that if John sings, it's probably mostly a Lennon song, and if Paul sings, then it's more likely a McCartney. Of greater significance for us, however, is the growing indication that McCartney tended to play bass with a different approach on Lennon's songs compared to his own.

Generally, McCartney is busier and more likely to take chances on a Lennon song (and, later, on Harrison's) while on his own songs he plays in a more restrained, even conventional way. It's certainly not a firm rule that applies to every single song, but it does happen often enough to imply a general working method, conscious or otherwise. Of course, Lennon and McCartney each wrote quite different kinds of songs when they worked on their own. George Martin said Lennon described his own method as "doing little bits which you then join up" and would go on to work his melody through the chords, whereas McCartney might come up with a melody first and then find the chords to fit it.[23]

Lennon explained in 1964: "None of us reads music. A melody idea may come first or an idea for the lyric may be first. Anyway, we noodle around with the instruments until we get a tune set that fits the words we want to use. We work hard at this. We've found that sometimes a song that sounds all right when delivered from a stage in a theatre lacks something when it comes to recording it."[24] Lennon hints here that they'd already grasped how recordings could be more creatively rewarding than live shows. This would in time change the course of the group's career.

Meanwhile, there was undoubtedly competition between Lennon and McCartney, especially when it came to bagging the new single. This is what is known as creative tension: productive for fans, infuriating for anyone close by. Maybe McCartney felt it wouldn't do any harm if he experimented and played more openly across a Lennon song, but for his own he wanted to keep the arrangement just so, to do 110 per cent for the record. On a song of his own, he's thinking of the lead vocal, he's thinking of backing vocals, what Ringo's doing, all the other elements, whereas the bass part he might well consider last. Maybe with John's songs he thought he had to make a bigger contribution to balance things out, which meant a strong bass part.

The songwriting on *Hard Day's Night* makes it primarily a Lennon album – and it would follow from our theory that the bass playing should be generally more expansive and interesting. So let's listen to four key songs, all by Lennon. 'I'm Happy Just to Dance With You' is a satisfying example of McCartney's blues-based playing, but listen in particular to the way he pushes the melodic ideas. There are counter-melodies everywhere. He's playing much more than if this had been his own song.

Then there's 'I'll Cry Instead', which contains the first example on record of McCartney being given the space to play a bass break – albeit under Lennon's vocal. He throws in a lovely phrase at 1:05 and then again at 1:35:

■ 'I'll Cry Instead'

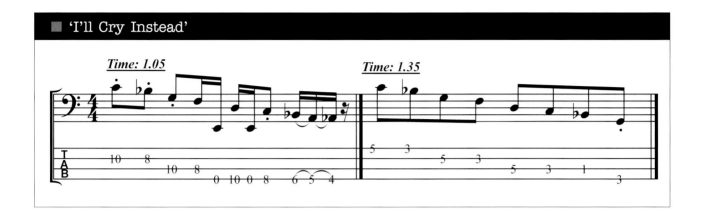

■ 'You Can't Do That'

See 'I'LL CRY INSTEAD' above

"Most of the figures that I have used on our records are not new," he said at the time. "I am certain that I have picked up many of them from listening to American rhythm and blues discs, but I do agree that basically I always try and work with Ringo during a recording session. We are the rhythm section and it's up to us to give the beat and punch to a disc."[25]

Certainly his head was full of America as they made Lennon's 'You Can't Do That': it was almost the first thing the group did upon returning from those ground-breaking *Ed Sullivan* TV shows in February and was aimed to fill the B-side of the next single, 'Can't Buy Me Love'. It was Harrison's 21st birthday too, and 'You Can't Do That' captures a happy quartet in understandably uproarious, exultant mood, not least that funky bass. It's a glorious early example of the funk in McCartney's bass work – and note that fill, first heard at 0:10:

See 'YOU CAN''T DO THAT' previous page

Our fourth Lennon song from *Hard Day's Night* is 'I Should Have Known Better', and here McCartney comes in deliberately late on a chord change. It stands out, for sure, and almost sounds like a mistake the first time it happens: the chord changes from G to E-minor at 0:17 but McCartney doesn't shift until a second later. He's exercising the bass's power of control, and when you get used to the effect as it recurs (0:35, 1:19, 1:37, 1:56) it becomes a statement, momentarily suspending movement.

"I started to realise the power the bass player had within the band. Not vengeful power, just that you could actually control it," explains McCartney. "As time went on, I began to realise that you didn't have to just play the root notes. If it was C, F, G then it was normally C, F, G that I played. But I started to realise that you could be pulling on that G, or just stay on the C when it went into F – things like that. And then I took it beyond that. I thought well, if you can do that, what else could you do? How much further could you take it? You might even be able to play notes that aren't in the chord. I just started to experiment."[26]

Contrast the bass on our fine *Hard Day's Night* quartet of Lennon songs with McCartney's work on some of his own songs on that album. Yes, he fills some of the space of 'And I Love Her' with appropriate double-stops, but it's precise and to the point, and on 'Things We Said Today' he tailors a controlled, unobtrusive part into his song. 'Can't Buy Me Love' was the first Beatles single with only one singer and it's clearly a McCartney song; he manages to sound merely like a singer who happens to play bass – a rare occurrence indeed.

Back in the USA, the group were building on their early successes to spearhead the so-called British Invasion. They were recorded at a concert at the Hollywood Bowl in Los Angeles in August 1964 for a proposed live album. Already the stage-show lagged behind what the group and their recording team were up to in the studio. Some of the tapes from the LA date were finally released in 1977 on *The Beatles At The Hollywood Bowl* (along with some further recordings made at the same venue the following year). Playing his regular 'number 2' Hofner through the AC-100 rig, and despite some variable recording quality on the American 3-track machine, McCartney is wonderfully confident. Check out the vibe on 'Roll Over Beethoven' or 'She Loves You' and note how on 'Boys' in particular he opens up the song and pushes himself and the group with some unusual fills and a strident pulse.

■ 'Eight Days A Week' 1

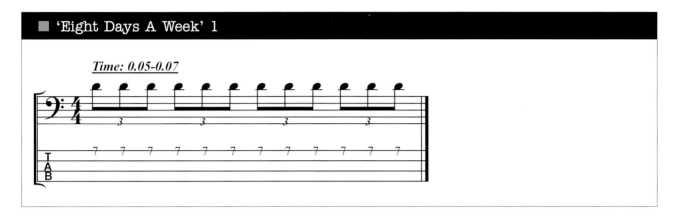

■ 'Eight Days A Week' 2

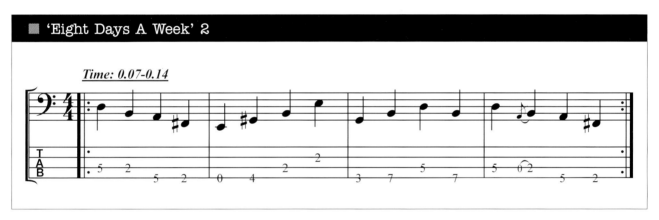

The fourth album, *Beatles For Sale*, is a disappointment after *Hard Day's Night*. The songs were mostly written in grabbed moments during a series of tours and then quickly recorded in between more gigs, from August to October 1964. Listening now, the bass playing sounds like a regression as the group balance uneasily on the treadmill. They sound like they had no time to do anything properly. The record has a poor mix and a weak overall sound. The best thing that can be said is that it's not their fault.

It's not that the bass playing on *Beatles For Sale* is bad. For example, on 'Eight Days A Week' check those opening triplets (0:05-0:07):

See 'EIGHT DAYS A WEEK' 1 above

and the easy groove of the walking line that follows:

See 'EIGHT DAYS A WEEK' 2 above

But there's too little to remind you that there's a world-class bassist at work on this album. An illustrative moment came during the sessions for 'What You're

WHAT YOU'RE DOING

Doing'. A few seconds into take ten McCartney plays a lurching fill that stops everyone in their tracks. He calls up to George Martin in the control room: "George, what did it sound like with the bass doing a funny thing? Did it sound any good or did it sound just utterly crap?" The diplomatic producer replies: "It sounded rather magnificent." The group are less charitable. As they prepare to start another take, Harrison urges: "Don't do it when we're singing." Then a disgruntled Lennon scowls: "Don't do it while we're playing." The vibe seems to be: we're in a hurry, Paul, so just do what's required and let's get this album out of the way. If that really was the attitude, it wouldn't last much longer.

At the end of the *For Sale* sessions they made a new single, 'I Feel Fine' / 'She's A Woman', and for the B-side McCartney let rip with a big, aggressive bass sound. After more than six minutes of a meandering jam on take seven, underpinned by the bassline, Ringo declared: "We've got a song and an instrumental there!" The version they made a few weeks later for the BBC was in some ways better than the (conventional length) take six released on the single. The Beeb cut, later included on the *Beatles Live At The BBC* collection, has exceptional phrasing and poise from McCartney.

We know that McCartney always had his antennae up for good bass playing and sounds coming from America. He absorbed and adapted the bass work he heard on records by countless (mainly black) artists on labels like Chess, Motown, Stax, Atlantic, and others. Resident in London since 1963, he heard those inspiring sounds regularly in the hip clubs there: it was an important part of any club's individual prestige to play the latest American records. And by now the group had made sure that Brian Epstein's Beatles USA company packaged up and sent over the latest American chart entries every month for them to pore over.

Probably in one batch around November 1964 McCartney would have pounced on Marvin Gaye's Tamla 45 'How Sweet It Is (To Be Loved By You)', which made the British charts the following month on the Stateside label. Without knowing his name, McCartney had discovered James Jamerson. Jamerson was the leading house bassman at the Motown studio in Detroit, and that latest single from Marvin Gaye had signs of how good Jamerson could be. He'd been evident on earlier records, but this was one of the first where he made the bass a prominent, melodic, and irreplaceable part of a Motown arrangement. McCartney's ears pricked up at the sound of a beautiful player at work in the grooves.

"I started listening to other bass players, and mainly Motown," says McCartney.

"As time went on James Jamerson became my hero, although I didn't actually know his name until quite recently. Jamerson and later Brian Wilson of The Beach Boys were my two biggest influences: James because he was so good and melodic, and Brian because he went to very unusual places."[27] It was around this time that Brian Wilson had started to use session bassists for Beach Boys records, including Carol Kaye and Ray Pohlman.

Jamerson's kinetic finger-funk wouldn't really happen as far as the general public were concerned until late 1966. Jamerson's influence on McCartney was inevitable – no 1960s bassist with ears could have missed him – but it's still questionable how much technical information McCartney could have picked up without ever seeing Jamerson play in the flesh. As he listened to the bass on those Motown records, the Beatles bassist would surely have absorbed some inspiration as he checked Jamerson's use of varied musical colours, and probably felt a competitive edge as he heard how effective it could be to take more chances. But actual instruction? No. In that sense James Jamerson was not as fundamental nor as all-encompassing an influence on McCartney as some might suggest or he himself recalls.

Meanwhile, in the Beatles camp in 1965 it was time for *Help!*. George Martin has since described the film-linked fifth album as a very rushed piece of work, and it certainly sounds that way. It was recorded in March and April. A well-known sign of their hectic recording regime was that they made the screeching rocker 'I'm Down' and the soothing ballad 'Yesterday' during the same day's session. How did they cope with that kind of schedule? "The answer is we just had to," McCartney shrugs. "Just did it. Sing the rocker, that's done: sing the ballad. And you seemed to have plenty of time for it. It's that law where whatever time they give you is enough. We had to be there at 10:00am, ready to go at 10:30. So you'd let yourselves in, test your amps, get yourselves in tune, which didn't take long. As long as you knew you weren't going to fart around, it takes about half an hour to do that."[28]

As the group aimed to squeeze out a couple of songs or more in a day, there was no time for philosophising. As McCartney puts it, nobody had a cup of tea and sat around to think about what to do. "You'd immediately walk over to the piano with George Martin and he'd say, 'What was the melody you were singing Paul?' I remember 'Yes It Is' because John would sing the melody and we'd have harmony lines all over the bloody place, but it was great: you each had to learn this new tune. And then George would have another tune. Really quite cool. But we were just used to doing it, so the minute we all sang it together it was oh, oh, that's good! And we'd sometimes stray to each other's lines, but we had enough discipline. It was like yeah, we can do this."[29]

The group's abilities with vocal harmonies spilled over into the way they made their instruments work together. They were experienced and skilled at interweaving vocal lines, and they easily made the same impact with their efforts on guitars and drums and bass and keyboards. Intelligent use of counter-melody was a Beatles speciality, whether they were singing or playing. The bass benefited greatly from this musical cross-pollination.

The most interesting song on *Help!* for bass playing is 'You're Going To Lose That Girl', a Lennon song where, once again, McCartney is motivated to contribute a more spontaneous part than if it had been his own song. But it's hardly his finest moment. Elsewhere, there are hints of that funkier influence, from Jamerson and others, such as his work on the title track, and there are some more double-stops to fill out the otherwise sparse arrangement on 'You've Got To Hide Your Love Away'.

Unreleased at the time, 'If You've Got Trouble' (included on 1996's *Anthology 2*) has a prominent unison guitar-and-bass riff that drives along the Ringo-vocal song. And while McCartney's bass-drone approach to the verse of 'Ticket To Ride' was novel, it was scuppered by poor sound on the record. He obviously liked the idea – and would apply it with better results later. But in hindsight *Help!* feels like a transitional record.

They were still gigging like crazy. A set of recordings was made once more at the group's Hollywood Bowl concerts in Los Angeles in August 1965 but, like the tapes from last year, they were not released at the time, lying around until 1977's *The Beatles At The Hollywood Bowl* LP. The results are much better than you'd expect from a severely under-amplified group generally fed up with live shows and overwhelmed by the racket from hordes of screaming kids. That same month, introducing a performance of 'Help!' to a British concert audience, Lennon announced: "Here's our latest record, or our latest electronic noise, depending on whose side you're on."

George Martin and his team did a good job on the Hollywood Bowl tapes in '77: have a listen to McCartney breezing through the difficult job of singing and playing 'She's A Woman' and 'Can't Buy Me Love', and listen in wonder at the juggernaut of a stacked-up riff that drives 'Dizzy Miss Lizzy' to a frenzy. McCartney had established that the bass was an important contributor to the Beatle sound. Now he was about to move up a gear and capture on record the best playing of his life.

A rare live date in 1966 as the studio years begin

the great recordings

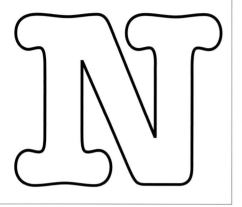

ow we move on to *Rubber Soul* – and now we start to get to the good stuff! From here on, and for the next few years, McCartney would dazzle fellow players with his instinct for great basslines and his knack for taking the bass guitar to ever-higher levels of achievement.

The group's sixth album was recorded in October and November 1965, as ever at Abbey Road and on a 4-track machine. In fact, Abbey Road engineers had started to find ways to get as much from the 4-track format as possible. Sometimes they filled three tracks and then mixed or 'reduced' them to the fourth track, or mixed a full 4-track down to one or two tracks of a second machine. Both methods provided more space for further overdubs to be added.

It's on *Rubber Soul* that McCartney makes his first consistent statement as a top-flight bassman. His playing is full of exuberance and enjoyment. Change was in the air – along with a strong whiff of marijuana – and during these sessions the group made a conscious effort to be different. There had been seeds of this on the earlier records, but the new album marked out The Beatles as musical innovators who were absorbing elements of folk, Indian, soul music, and more into the pop framework. "We always thought The Supremes were a bit boring, it always sounded like the same song almost, or very near," says McCartney. "They were trying to *keep* the Motown-Supremes sound. Well, we always *weren't* trying to keep the Beatles sound. We were always trying to move on. We were always trying to get a new sound on every single thing we did."[30]

McCartney had a new sound available in the shape of the Rickenbacker bass that he'd acquired on a recent American tour. The California-based manufacturer, delighted by Lennon and Harrison's use of their guitars, gave him a new left-handed Rickenbacker 4001S bass guitar, which he started using straight away for the *Rubber Soul* sessions. He says that from that album onwards "it could have easily swung either way" between using the Hofner or the Rickenbacker in the studio, although the Rickenbacker does seem to have quickly become his preferred studio instrument.

He continued to use his Hofner on stage, where it had become an identifiable part of the group's image. "I was known for the violin shape," he says. "It's like Charlie Chaplin, you know? The little walking cane, little moustache, and a bowler hat, and he's Charlie. If he comes on with a bandanna and he's shaved and he's on a bike, it's like: 'Who's that?' So I think there may have been an element of the Hofner being a stage trademark. Also it was very light and I'd always played it live, so I might have been playing safe a bit, just using the instrument I'd always used."[51]

He remembers being given the Rickenbacker. "Oh, great! Freebie. Thank you very much! But it's very difficult to remember much off the Beatle tours, because when you weren't playing you were off, and you were either being whisked around or having a party. Actually remembering it the morning after was difficult, to remember what you'd done, never mind 40 years after."[52]

McCartney says that the long-scale Rickenbacker felt different and stayed in tune better than the Hofner. "It sounded a little clearer, too," he recalls, "and seemed a little heavier; not just literally heavier, but it played a little more solid than the Hofner. ... Tuning had been a major problem with the Hofner. Usually the E could be in tune but the third-fret G on that string was always a little bit sharp, so as soon as you'd gone to the third fret you were out. I liked everything about it, but it was embarrassing if you weren't quite in tune for something, you know?"[53]

The Rickenbacker 4001S has a longer scale-length than the Hofner 500/1, which means the string tension is tighter, in turn giving a better focus to each note and improved overall sustain, providing a more tangible bass-end to the sound, in contrast to the warm, woody thud of the Hofner. The change of instrument happened as the recording technology was improving too, a happy coincidence, and for studio amplifiers McCartney had his Vox AC-100 and a new Fender Bassman rig to choose between. 'I'm Looking Through You' on *Rubber Soul* is a good example of the sonic changes. There's a low growl in the bass, and the sound sits in a contained, tightly defined area. It's almost as if we're hearing McCartney's excitement at the new tones available to him; it's all about tone, and suddenly there's a lot more bass-end. There's even a coincidentally suitable lyric line in the song itself: "The only difference is you're down there."

'Drive My Car' was among the earliest tracks recorded for the new album, and what an opener it made for the record. American singles, especially from black artists, were still having a big impact on the group. Perhaps that partly explains

Rubber Soul's punning title? As ever, they looked forward to the monthly package of new American goodies shipped over from Beatles USA, and must have flipped when they heard Otis Redding's 'Respect' with Duck Dunn's lovely bass part. It came out almost the week they recorded 'Drive My Car' and surely must have inspired the bassline. But wherever it started, McCartney made the line on that track entirely his own. The bass immediately announces itself, with a big, rounded bottom end, doubled by guitar. (See full transcription and analysis, page 82.)

George Harrison's 'If I Needed Someone', made in October 1965, marks the start of the group's psychedelic approach to their music. There is a spacey, open feel to what McCartney plays in the verses, a pedal riff that holds the piece together. ('Pedal' means the effect when a bass note is deliberately repeated or sustained against changing harmony.)

Photographs from the session for this song show McCartney with a capo on his Rickenbacker.[34] Capos are used by guitarists, rarely by bassists. The movable little device is fitted over the strings and the fingerboard, behind a fret, shortening the length of the strings and therefore raising the pitches. Guitarists usually use a capo to transpose a song into a singer-friendly key. So why would a bass player use one? Shown the photo, McCartney laughs in bemusement: "What am I doing there?" After some fruitless thought, he continues: "Well, the thing with the bass on a lot of this stuff was that you'll try anything once. So I'll try a capo on a bass. ... I would just mess around with any experimental effects." He gives up. "I'd try anything!"[35]

Our theory is that McCartney probably wanted to create a 'drone' type of bassline, in keeping with the psychedelic feel that underpins 'Someone'. He wanted a low A in the line, but used the capo to avoid playing it as an open string or at the fifth fret of his E string. The open A would have had too much of an aggressive, cutting edge; the E-string fretted note would have left him a long way from his target zone, requiring an annoyingly large leap across the frets. Instead, fitting the capo at the fifth fret frees him to comfortably play the higher melodic segment of the bassline up by the tenth fret, an area of the neck that provides the naturally softer and smoother sounding tone that he wants for his dreamy drone.

Rubber Soul is an album where the group exploit their freedom to try different and new ideas, and so it is for the bass. If you've successfully adopted one device usually reserved for guitar, the capo, then why not another, the fuzz box? That's exactly what McCartney does on 'Think For Yourself', playing a very guitar-like

distorted bass part throughout (stereo right), which he bolsters with an overdubbed regular bass (stereo left) that more or less doubles the fuzz part.

'Michelle' is a beautiful piece of bass playing, with McCartney paying microscopic attention to his phrasing and note lengths. It's still a groove that does the job of moving the song along, but you sense that taste and feel are everything for him here. The bassline offers a secondary melody alongside the vocal, and one that is just as interesting and memorable. He doesn't need to play much to achieve the effect he needs, which points to the speed at which his arranger's ear and sensitivity were developing.

In fact, 'Michelle' is a solo McCartney effort. (The group had been in Manchester the previous day for a TV performance, so maybe everyone else stayed over after a heavy night?) McCartney recalls that he didn't know what he would do for the bassline on 'Michelle' until the session itself came around. "That was actually thought up on the spot," he says. "I would never have played 'Michelle' on bass until I had to record the bassline. Bass isn't an instrument you sit around and sing to. I don't, anyway. But I remember that opening six-note phrase against the descending chords in 'Michelle', that was like, oh, a great moment in my life. I think I had enough musical experience after years of playing, and off of my dad, so it was just in me. I just realised I could do that. It's quite a well known trick – I'm sure jazz players have done that against a descending sequence – but wherever I got it from, somewhere in the back of my brain said: 'Do that, it's a bit cleverer for the arrangement, and it'll really sound good on those descending chords.'"[56]

Another bass highlight on *Rubber Soul* occurs with 'Nowhere Man'. In a part full of movement you can hear the melodic hooks coming together as McCartney feeds ideas into his bassline from the vocal melody. He's becoming a careful and responsive listener, a key skill for any musician who wants to move beyond the merely good.

'You Won't See Me' is the pinnacle of McCartney's early pop bass style (see full transcription and analysis, page 104). In an improvisatory frame of mind, he grounds the part in what he knows will work but adds plenty of individual colour and shading as the piece moves forward. Even with a song like 'What Goes On', where it sounds as if he's simply using more of the old ideas, he lifts things with the walking-bass idea. On this album his execution is more precise, his sound is clearer, and his technique is a great deal better. Which of course means his playing benefits. Best of all, he's quite clearly enjoying himself.

THE WORD

On 'In My Life' we hear a world-class rhythm section at work playing one of the finest grooves they ever recorded. Just sit back and wonder at the feel between the bass and the kit. It is, quite simply, a beautiful two minutes and 23 seconds. (See full transcription and analysis, page 90.)

And if you thought that was good, let's move on to 'The Word'. Any bass players of the time who hadn't already twigged that this was a very important bassist were about to have their minds blown, man. This is McCartney being seriously and originally funky. Where did it come from? Well, you have to conclude that it's from his own fervent musical imagination. (See full transcription and analysis, page 96.)

On some *Rubber Soul* songs it's the sheer simplicity of what McCartney plays that is impressive. Often it can be a more difficult task – and reflects greater discipline – for a player to do less. Some musicians take a long time to realise that there can be as much value to what you don't play as to what you do play. For the waltz-time 'Norwegian Wood' McCartney scores with simplicity by decorating some of the gaps and playing off the vocal melody, and similarly with 'Girl', another of his object lessons in the effectiveness of pure simplicity. McCartney knows as much as anyone that there is a great deal of satisfaction to be had from a simple part perfectly executed.

In more recent times there has been a move among some players to high levels of technical accomplishment and what we might call over-playing. We can probably all think of bassists whose chops, for want of a less competitive word, are spectacular but whose outpourings leave us colder than a winter morning. The ability to play challenging melodic and rhythmic phrases or to deploy a great number of awkwardly juxtaposed notes in a very short space of time does not necessarily equal innovation or longevity. Those skills are only a small percentage of the whole package. Bass players need to play solidly, consistently, and evenly, at any given tempo, without speeding up or slowing down, and, to cut through one annoying piece of folklore, they shouldn't rely solely on someone else – that's right, the drummer – to hold everything together. The best players have a good feel or groove, a talent that relates to where, specifically, they place their notes against each point that we call a beat. Simplicity can be one of the greatest musical virtues, and a good bass player will be well aware of this.

Back to 1965, and during the *Rubber Soul* sessions the group recorded both sides of their next single, 'Day Tripper' / 'We Can Work It Out'. 'Tripper' was dashed off in an afternoon and sounds like something of a regression amid the

invention of the album tracks, with the group reshaping the riff from Roy Orbison's 'Oh Pretty Woman', a hit from the previous September. The single's flipside, 'We Can Work It Out', is better, with some funky bass ideas, although the poor sound doesn't help.

Then came a long break for the group – at last! – interrupted only by a nine-date British tour at the end of 1965. The Beatles would not tour the UK again. They would not record again until April 1966. It would be well worth the wait.

The Beatles spent more time than they'd ever spent before on an album when they came to record *Revolver*, made between April and June 1966. With the success of the diverse *Rubber Soul* behind them, they were determined to make this one the best they could – and probably already had it in mind that they would soon stop playing live altogether. The studio had become their natural habitat. They wanted to make more effective recordings that drew on all their skills and made the most of the people and gear at their disposal at Abbey Road studios.

They now had a fresh new engineer, too, in Geoff Emerick, at 20 unusually young for such a job by EMI standards (and four years younger than McCartney). He would help to bring a new clarity and depth to the group's sound, especially the bass and drums, and along with George Martin provided new opportunities for risk-taking that the group would seize upon.

The first recording they made after their break – the first since the final *Rubber Soul* sessions back in November – was 'Tomorrow Never Knows'. McCartney drew on his earlier experiments on 'Ticket To Ride' and concentrated on providing a bass drone. This time it worked. It's another example of McCartney's discipline, his ability to restrain his playing. It's of immense importance to know when *not* to take the opportunity to play more than is necessary, even with a wide open space in front of you. He no longer has to prove that he's a clever bassman. Simple can be clever too.

Well, sometimes, anyway. They recorded a new single early in the album sessions, 'Paperback Writer' / 'Rain'. It was around this time that Geoff Emerick began grappling with the group's request to try to get more bass-end on to tape. Emerick recalled using a loudspeaker as a microphone to soak up more bass frequencies than a regular mic could manage. (A loudspeaker and a microphone are both transducers: in other words, they are devices that convert one form of energy into another. Emerick simply reversed the properties of the loudspeaker, making it sense air vibrations and convert those to an electrical signal.) Sometimes

Emerick has remembered doing this for 'Paperback Writer'[57] or for "two tracks on *Revolver*".[58] 'Paperback Writer' and 'Rain' were recorded during the *Revolver* sessions, so it was probably those two he was thinking of. And what a bass on both!

American records still seemed to have bigger, bolder bass. John Lennon wondered aloud to an Abbey Road engineer why "a certain Wilson Pickett record"[39] had more bottom-end than any of the Beatles discs (maybe 'In The Midnight Hour', a September 1965 UK hit for Pickett). "We were listening to these records, like the ones from Tamla, and there was all that extra bass-end," said Emerick. "And we were always [wondering how they got] that sound. Now, a lot of it was the musicianship, of course. But there was no one to tell us these things; we had to find out by our own methods. It was the amount of bass and also the level – the loudness – that fascinated us. You see, there were certain things that we weren't allowed to do [at Abbey Road]. There were limitations on how much bass we were allowed to have on."[40] The irony was that, by now, many American engineers and musicians were in awe of the sound coming from Abbey Road and other key London studios in the 1960s, with one of the main attractions being what one top US producer called "the great, thin British vocal sound".[41]

In pursuit of better bass-end, Emerick rigged up his speaker-turned-mic. "And that was the bass sound for the 'Paperback Writer' single, which was really, for its time, incredible. No one had heard the power of a bass, certainly on an English record, like that."[42] Abbey Road engineer Tony Clark cut the 'Paperback Writer' / 'Rain' single, which he remembered later as EMI's first high-level cut. Emerick: "I remember the buzz that quickly went around Abbey Road when it became apparent what we had achieved with the sound of a record. People were standing outside the door and listening. It was so different."[43]

Aside from the big sound, McCartney's playing on the A-side, 'Paperback Writer', is something of a template for his work in a rockier context, kicking into a solid, rhythmic, root-note groove with some added colour en route. Check out the lovely high-register fills at 0:12 and 1:50:

See 'PAPERBACK WRITER' opposite

And then there was the B-side, 'Rain' (see full transcription and analysis, page 112). This was something else altogether. Perhaps it's the bastard son of 'If I Needed Someone', or maybe it's McCartney reaching back to Johnny Kidd's 'Shakin' All Over' for note choice and inspiration. But it's where he takes it that

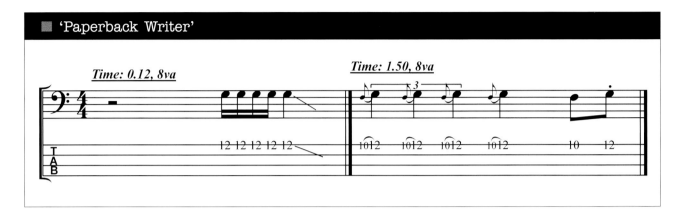

matters. 'Rain' is full-throttle, hell-for-leather, take-no-prisoners bass. It's shocking; it's exciting; it's sheer joyful bass playing. We challenge any bass player to listen hard to this virtuosic piece of work and not be smiling almost all the way through. And it's a Lennon song, with McCartney again at his most free and most spontaneous. The drums aren't half bad either.

Years later Ringo said: "I think it's the best out of all the records I've ever made. 'Rain' blows me away. It's out of left field. I know me and I know my playing – and then there's 'Rain'."[44] McCartney: "Lots of things you see about The Beatles now don't even mention Ringo. Oh, wasn't he the drummer chappy? And he was so central; the four of us were absolutely necessary for that band. Integral, really."[45]

Experimentation went further than fiddling with the miking-up. During the *Revolver* sessions the Abbey Road team began to look deeper into the creative possibilities of varispeeding, and 'Rain' was an early beneficiary of the technique. Varispeeding means changing the speed of the tape recorder: the technicians rigged up a control knob that could change the speed at which the tape ran. A week or so earlier while recording 'Tomorrow Never Knows' the group had been enchanted by the sound that slowed-down instruments assumed. So they decided to apply the same ideas to 'Rain'. They performed the backing track faster than they would have done naturally, with the 4-track running faster than normal too. When the recording was played back at regular speed, the tempo slowed down to how they would normally have played it, but now the sound had that deeper, darker quality they wanted. McCartney said: "We got a big, ponderous, thunderous backing and then we worked on top of that as normal, so that it didn't sound like a slowed-down thing: it just had a big ominous noise to it."[46]

A couple of days after they recorded that instrumental backing there was a further session for various overdubs, apparently including bass. The released 'Rain' sounds almost in G; the instrumental backing was probably recorded in A, varispeeded to G (down a tone). The bass sounds occasional low Ds, a tone below the usual lowest note on the E string, at bars 23, 24, and 66 (0:47, 0:49, and 2:24). There are two main possibilities to explain how the bass arrived on the recording. McCartney may have recorded his bass as part of the instrumental backing on the first day, so that what you hear on the record is him playing his bass in concert pitch varispeeded down a tone. The other possibility is that he recorded no bass the first day but overdubbed the full part on the second day. Possibly this was done with the tape running at normal speed and his bass tuned down a tone, or with the tape running at the reduced speed and his bass tuned to concert pitch. Got that? One further possibility is that on the second day he recorded his bass against the normal-speed backing with his E string simply tuned down to D – and this is what we have assumed for our full transcription (see page 112).

The group made 'Rain' into a deliberately bass-led concoction. They must have intended the bass guitar to be the lead instrument on the song: it was played that way, recorded that way, and mixed that way. "I may have compressed the bass two or even three times," said Emerick, "just to give it no dynamic range whatsoever and get it way out front."[47] A compressor is an electronic studio gadget that smoothes the sound of an instrument or voice, making quiet sounds louder and louder sounds quieter. He added: "I used to try to pull the bass out of the track to get its own space, and hear it more defined. And one way I tried to do it was to put a tiny bit of chamber [reverberation] on it. I started to do that on *Revolver*, but Paul could always detect even the slightest amount, and he wouldn't accept it. So I had to be careful."[48]

Work on *Revolver* continued. On Harrison's 'Taxman' (see full transcription and analysis, page 120) McCartney is again in high spirits for the bass, opting not to take the easy way out at this fierce tempo and instead creating a dominating, powerful line with incessant sixteenth-note pounding and some inspired use of space. There's yet more influence here from the American singles the group loved to hear, notably the feel of James Brown's 'I Got You (I Feel Good)' – with Bernard Odum on bass, and a British hit right at this time. McCartney was starting to play guitar in the studio more, too, and his fine solo on this song echoes the octave jump of his bass riff.

Revolver is chock full of great bass playing, with McCartney mostly on the

Rickenbacker through the Fender Bassman or some new Vox solid-state amps. Try the sleazy, lazy groove of Lennon's 'I'm Only Sleeping' (see full transcription and analysis, page 128), a medium-tempo shuffle with an underlying funk and full of good ideas, especially in the choruses. Or Lennon's 'She Said She Said', with the bass often following the shape of the vocal, playing off and around it to create fascinating counter-melodies. McCartney demonstrates his growing feel for space, with tight control of note placement and lengths, and he meshes well with the drums. In the 3/4 bridge ("When I was a boy...") he plays a little more safely, hitting quarter-notes to mark the beats. (He told Barry Miles years later[49] that, following a studio argument, Harrison played bass on 'She Said', but that seems unlikely on the evidence of the released version. Surely this is pure McCartney?)

McCartney's work on Lennon's 'And Your Bird Can Sing' contributes a good deal to this little gem, another in the spontaneous bass style of 'Rain' and 'Taxman'. It's a superb piece of expansive, melodic playing with a classy funk-pop verse – more James in his head, perhaps, whether Jamerson or Brown – and some neat hammer-ons and clever scalar movement. The result is a line that happily mixes the traditional with his new busier approach. An out-take of an earlier (and very jolly) version, released on *Anthology 2*, reveals some nice fills in a different part pitched against the original rolling melody.

There's more gorgeous melodic bass playing on his own 'For No One'. McCartney plays with beautiful execution, again working off the vocal line – itself one of his more playful and unusual melodies. His tone and approach are almost that of an orchestral player, as if he were the bottom end of a horn section, an impression encouraged by the presence of that famous French horn solo – which was McCartney's idea. We'll hear more of this 'tuba' approach later.

On 'For No One' his bass part is carefully considered and constructed, with an arranger's ear hard at work and the impression that he's playing a role. There's no question of 'adding' something with the bass: it's an integral part of an overall arrangement. (The first take of 'For No One' reveals McCartney on solo piano, with one of his later bass licks already evident in his piano part, implying that he'd probably identified it as an important motif early in the song's life.) More good bass for one of his own songs comes with 'Got To Get You Into My Life' and its simple, effective part. Listen to the opening pedal sequence in the verse and a fabulous little triplet lick, first heard at 0:17:

See 'GOT TO GET YOU INTO MY LIFE' next page

'Got To Get You Into My Life'

Time: 0.17

Then there's the descending chorus line. McCartney's bassline is all about the drive he provides, with purposefully clipped quarter-notes and tight overall control. After the guitar breakdown he opens up the pedal line with a glorious series of double-stops and triplets, heading into the fade.

As for the rest of *Revolver*, even when McCartney gets functional, as on 'Doctor Robert', the impressive improvements in his execution and sound are still evident. The Rickenbacker was coming into its own. He's solid and powerful on 'Good Day Sunshine', intentionally matching the bass end of the piano and slipping into an odd time pre-fade, starting at 1:42.

In 'I Want To Tell You' he stays deliberately static until the third verse when he again displays a tasteful laidback technique, harking back to the Jamerson of 'How Sweet It Is'. Even on 'Yellow Submarine', where you might expect Ringo-song ordinariness, there's a beautifully constructed bassline. McCartney was revelling in his craftsmanship. "That's really what I enjoy," he admits. "I enjoy the craft of it."[50]

And the craft was about to hit an ever greater high. The group played what turned out to be their final and generally dispiriting concerts in Europe, Japan, The Philippines, and the USA, grinding to a halt at San Francisco's Candlestick Park at the end of August 1966. They would no longer be a touring group. Some thought that this inevitably marked the end for The Beatles. But in November they began recording songs for a new album.

Sgt Pepper's Lonely Hearts Club Band is the best Beatles album McCartney made for consistently inventive basslines. *Rubber Soul* had promise, *Revolver* hit a lot of high marks, but *Pepper* does it virtually every time. On many of the *Pepper* songs, recorded from late 1966 into early 1967, it's the bass that is the dominant instrument. That's down to the way it's played, precisely what McCartney plays, the sound of his bass, and the instrument's prominence in the mix. Here's a bass player saying with confidence: this is my style now. He's aware he's in control, that he can turn on his creativity whenever he needs it or feels like it. And very often the results are startling.

Both sides of the single they released at the time, 'Strawberry Fields Forever' /

'Penny Lane', were originally intended for the album and were among the first things recorded for it. The bass on 'Strawberry Fields' is well played and functional, with a solid feel for phrasing and tone, filling a frequency area within a dense sound picture. 'Penny Lane', however, is a revelation. This is the new *Sgt Pepper* bass style! One of the most significant changes to McCartney's recording method now was that he would very often tape the bass late in the song's studio life. Delaying his commitment gave him time to compose an often ornate and always memorable bassline, free from the requirement to get it right from the start.

"I often used to record without the bass," he recalls of the *Pepper* sessions, "which George [Harrison] particularly used to get narked at. Because he'd say oh, it doesn't sound like a band. And I knew what he meant. But I'd written it on guitar [or piano] and I wanted to get the feel of how I'd written it, so I'd often say: 'Do you mind if we don't put the bass on? Pretend it's there, and it'll give me a chance to put in on after.'"[51]

Engineer Geoff Emerick remembered that during the time they made *Sgt Pepper* he'd often stay behind in the evenings with McCartney after everyone else had left – McCartney lived nearby at the time – and they'd record the bass part for a song already on tape. Emerick would take McCartney's bass amp, probably still the Fender Bassman or a Vox solid-state job, and move it out into the middle of Abbey Road's big studio 2.

The engineer wanted to get more of the room sound around the bass, and would set up his preferred AKG C-12 microphone, sometimes as much as eight feet away from the speaker cabinet and often in 'figure of eight' format. This switched the mic's response pattern so that it picked up as much from behind as in front, enhancing that room sound. Emerick would usually compress the bass, too, which as we've seen 'squeezes' the result so that the louder sounds are quieter and the quieter sounds louder, giving a smooth overall effect and bringing the bass guitar forward in the mix.

"You can hear on some of the *Pepper* tracks that there is a slightly different quality about the bass," said Emerick. "The original 4-track machines were one-inch [tape], so every track was a quarter-inch wide and there was no noise. The quality of the bass on those numbers was outstanding."[52] He added: "To me, at that time, it was the ultimate bass sound. I couldn't improve it."[53]

Emerick gave the bass another lift at the mixing stage. "When I was mixing – and [early Beatles engineer] Norman Smith taught me this – the last instrument you bring in is the bass. So through *Pepper* everything was mixed without hearing the bass. I used to bring everything to -2 on the VU meter and then bring the bass in and make it go to 0, so it meant the bass was 2dB louder than anything on the record. It was way out in front, the loudest thing on the record."[54]

Back to 'Penny Lane'. There were days of sessions for the song, first of all recording McCartney's multiple pianos, then vocals, then more piano, guitars, and vocals – and only then the bass and drums, followed by brass, woodwind, and bell overdubs and the famous solo trumpet. A number of 'reductions', or mixdowns, had to be made from one full 4-track to a single track of another so that all the necessary overdubs could be accommodated. The reborn Beatles, now a recording group only, were striding out into their new sound-world.

The bass playing on 'Penny Lane' is a classic McCartney conjunction: a beautiful, craftsmanlike job plus completely fresh ideas added along the way. It is a precursor of more good-taste basslines to come. Listen how he edges towards a counter-melody, contrasting the walking and non-walking sections.

But all that work to build up the instruments has made for a curious sound picture, the more peculiar the deeper you dig. Note the carefully deployed semitone trill on the bass, first at 0:10-0:17 and again later (for example at 0:59). And what about those double-stops at 0:42? Oddest of all, however, must be the bowed double-bass, audible (just) around 2:04. They brought in sessionman Frank Clarke to play this briefest of brief drop-ins. What on earth for? "They wanted me to play one note over and over, for hours," complained an exasperated Clarke.[55]

As they had on 'Rain', The Beatles and their studio team used varispeeding on the bass (and some other instruments) on 'Penny Lane', giving a very slightly speeded-up result. They did it again, in the other direction, for the bass on 'Lovely Rita' (see full transcription and analysis, page 136), with the released version ending up just sharp of E-flat. McCartney probably played the original part in E. And what a part! He goes back and forth between a triadic approach (using notes that form the chord) and a scalar approach (using notes from the parent scales). There's a great sense of exuberance and fun as the bass constantly moves the song along. It's clearly the principal melodic instrument here, a hallmark of so many *Pepper* songs. And before we leave 'Rita', have a listen to that wonderfully leftfield repeated phrase at the very end (from 2:12).

Can it get any better? On 'Getting Better' McCartney plays less overall than he might have done on a *Revolver*-era piece, although by the fourth and fifth choruses

he's subtly embellishing around the accents. But generally he recognises the different requirement here, and his arranger's ear keeps him in check most of the time. He's orchestrating the part, thinking carefully about the impact of what notes he should play, how he should shape them, and where precisely they should go. There's a bottom-end clarity helped by Emerick's late-night efforts with the middle-of-the-room amp and the compressor, and by the improved tone of the Rickenbacker. "Round about the time of *Sgt Pepper* I definitely was using the Rickenbacker quite a lot," says McCartney.[56]

A massive interval leap characterises the verse part of 'Getting Better' (two octaves, G-to-G, first heard at 0:08):

See 'GETTING BETTER' next page

This is about as big a jump as you can make on a four-string bass, and marks his increasing use of extreme range on the instrument, knowing that the Rick can handle it. More wonderful ideas stream from his bass on 'With A Little Help From My Friends'. This is lead bass playing! But it's not over-busy, nor is it extravagant for the sake of it. He works some tasteful licks around the vocal line, supporting and melodic in the verses, less colourful in the choruses. Again, you can tell that he's spent a good deal of thought on his note choices and how and where to play them. Listen especially for that high fill at 0:46:

See 'WITH A LITTLE HELP' next page

There's nothing flash or self-conscious about the tasteful bassline for 'Lucy In The Sky With Diamonds', a remarkable piece of bass work, especially the chorus groove, first heard from 0:56:

See 'LUCY IN THE SKY' next page

'Lucy' like most of this record's songs had the bass recorded relatively late. It took only two days to record this one, which counted as quick for *Pepper*. The group recorded a basic track on the first day, with drums but without bass, and then on day two added varispeeded vocals. A composite of early takes released on *Anthology 2* reveals the relatively complete yet bass-less picture. Only after all that was done was the carefully considered bass added, virtually the last piece of work to be recorded onto the multitrack tape.

"It was much better for me to work out the bass later, you know," McCartney said as he chatted to producer George Martin about 'Lucy' in a film on the making of *Sgt Pepper*. "The good thing about doing it later is it allowed me to get melodic bass lines." Martin agreed, saying: "All the bass lines were always very

WITH A LITTLE HELP FROM MY FRIENDS

■ 'Getting Better'

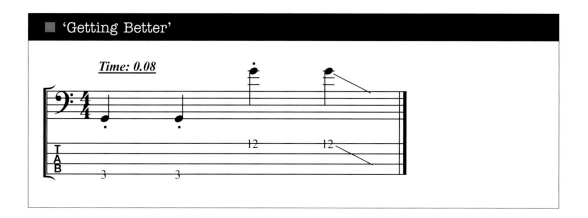

■ 'With A Little Help From My Friends'

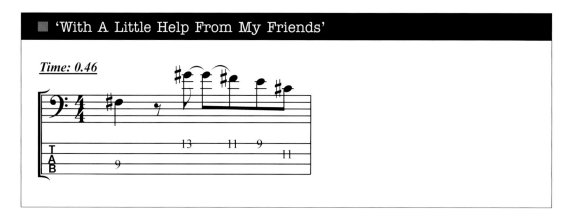

■ 'Lucy In The Sky With Diamonds'

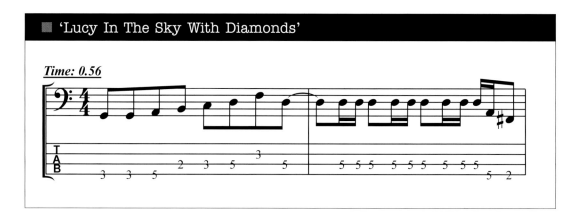

interesting," to which McCartney replied: "On this album I think that [adding the bass later] was one of the reasons."[57]

With pieces like 'Lucy' McCartney created his own personal bass style. He's not a jazz head, like James Jamerson at Motown, nor does he go mad like Jack Bruce or John Entwistle might have done with the same material. He was certainly aware of all those players, as ever listening widely and absorbing what was going on around him.

Jamerson was still doing remarkable things with his Fender Precision Bass. There are many classic bass parts in the Motown canon, not least Jamerson's work on Stevie Wonder's 'I Was Made to Love Her', 'Reach Out' by The Four Tops, and 'You Keep Me Hangin' On' by The Supremes. Entwistle, at work in The Who, had come to fellow musicians' notice at the end of 1965 with his astonishing bass breaks on 'My Generation', and was continuing to shake up the bass ground. Bruce defined a new style of rock bass playing on Cream's extended live outings, a direction followed with relish by Phil Lesh of The Grateful Dead and Jack Casady in Jefferson Airplane.

But McCartney had defined the bassman's territory in the first place, and now he'd found his own distinctive voice, one with which he spoke loudly and clearly throughout *Sgt Pepper*. "It did become a lot more of a funky instrument," he says of his bass playing in the late 1960s. "It was becoming almost like a drum, the rhythmic possibilities. It was very exciting, that. And I became very proud to be the bass player in The Beatles."

He adds: "I was thinking that maybe I could even run a little tune through the chords that doesn't exist anywhere else. Maybe I can have an independent melody? *Sgt Pepper* ended up being my strongest thing on bass, the independent melodies. … On 'Lucy In The Sky With Diamonds', for example, you could easily have had root notes, it would be like 'Louie Louie' or something. Whereas I was playing an independent melody through it, a little tune through the chords that doesn't exist anywhere else, and that became my thing. It's only really a way of getting from C to F or whatever, but you get there in an interesting way. … It was all very exciting.

"Once you realised the control you had over the band, you were in control. They can't go anywhere, man. Ha! Power! I then started to identify with other bass players, [to] talk bass with the guys in the bands. In fact, when we met Elvis, he was trying to learn bass, so I was like: 'You're trying to learn bass are you … son? Sit down, let me show you a few things.' So I was very proud of being the bass player. As it went on and [I] got into that melodic thing, that was probably the peak of my interest."[58]

With 'Fixing A Hole' comes more evidence that McCartney was micro-managing his phrasing. Here he seems to want to be melodic but not complicated, to play an entirely suitable bassline that complements the song and ends up as if it is the only possible part that could have been played. (There has been a suggestion that this is Lennon playing bass.[59] Certainly it's not as well played as the rest of the record and has been less worked on – perhaps because it was recorded during the group's first session outside Abbey Road, at Regent studio, and is the only *Pepper* song where the bass wasn't put on later. We still think it's McCartney.)

Many of the *Pepper* lines, including 'Fixing A Hole', sound as if McCartney's intention may have been to create an almost tuba-like low-pitched horn tone and to place the instrument within the arrangement with that in mind. Interestingly, his grandfather had been in the local works brass-band playing an E-flat Bass, a large bass horn that sat below the bass trombone at the bottom end of the band instruments' range. Back in late 1965 a reporter was at Abbey Road with The Beatles as McCartney sent out roadie Mal Evans for "an E-flat brass bass". McCartney instructed Evans: "It's like a euphonium. You know, I think The Temperance Seven used to have one. I want it to give an oompha noise in one of the numbers."[60]

But now it was his bass guitar that provided plenty of oompha. Perhaps the need for that brassy tuba-like bass sound lurked somewhere in McCartney's genes? While we're on the subject, take a look at The Beatles on the *Sgt. Pepper* jacket. There they are, bedecked in what can only be described as bandstand gear. And one of the songs in the early Beatles live sets had been 'If You Gotta Make A Fool Of Somebody' – a cover of James Ray's 1961 original that had a tuba playing the bassline.

Back to *Pepper*, and in 'Good Morning Good Morning' the bass controls the rhythmic dynamics, driving the song forward, with a pleasing scalar run at 1:42:

See 'GOOD MORNING' opposite

There's a bootleg in circulation of the bare take eight that allows a useful insider's view of the bass-drums interplay. 'Being For The Benefit Of Mr Kite' is another *Pepper* track worth a careful listen. McCartney does a fine job as he starts to work with Lennon's vocal line, creating another assured example of what he calls his "independent melodies". And again the intention seems to be to simulate

a bass brass instrument in tone and purpose. When the song reaches the second cut-up fairground organ section, some of the organ bass clashes with the bass guitar (around 2:07), but the effects-less take seven included on *Anthology 2* affords an unencumbered view.

Anthology 2 also provides takes one and two of 'Kite', with Lennon evidently smashed out of his head. He was immersed in LSD at the time, and so McCartney seems largely to

have been running the show for this album. George Martin told an interviewer a few years later: "I suppose that, looking back on it, [*Pepper*] wouldn't have happened if the boys hadn't got into the drug scene. But I can also say that it wouldn't have happened if I hadn't been *not* on the drug scene, because if I hadn't been a normal person I don't think *Pepper* would ever have been formed in that way. I don't think it would have been coherent." The interviewer asked if Martin had to pull the group together for the recordings. "No, I just had to be patient. You can't do much with a guy when he's giggling all the time."[61]

If you had to play a non-believer just one Beatles album to prove that McCartney is a very good bass player indeed, it would have to be *Sgt Pepper*. It's all there and right up-front: the taste, the feel, the tone, the content, the ideas, the surprises, the smiles; the lot, in fact. It's impossible to imagine anyone else doing this at the time. Or even now. McCartney was 24, growing up and changing in his attitudes. And best of all, his group didn't have to tour any more. All his efforts went into the studio work. "I think there was a prize period when I was playing my best bass," he recalls. "I could concentrate everything on writing the song, singing harmony with John, or playing the bass. [That was] pretty much my role, or maybe playing a bit of piano or guitar or something. Other than that I really didn't have much to do, so you could put all your energy into that."[62]

Digging into the Rickenbacker for some psychedelic bass

1 9 6 7 - 1 9 7 0

and in the
end...

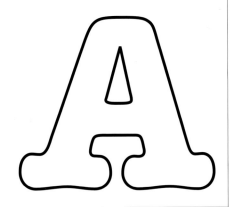

fter the highs of *Rubber Soul*, *Revolver*, and *Sgt Pepper*, it must have seemed at the time that anything was possible for McCartney and his bass in The Beatles. But the brilliance would not be sustained, although there were still some wonderful treats in store. The Beatles could have played some of the *Revolver* tracks live (although they never did). In contrast, the *Pepper* recordings were studio creations intended to go no further. And anyway, the group seemed to be saying, this wasn't The Beatles any more: it was Sgt Pepper's Lonely Hearts Club Band. After all that remarkable work, it was almost inevitable that there would be a void after *Sgt Pepper*. For the rest of 1967 the group seemed to slip. Maybe it was the drugs? It didn't help their stability when manager Brian Epstein died in August at the age of just 32.

'Only A Northern Song' is a *Pepper* out-take, not released until 1968's ragbag album, *Yellow Submarine*. Despite Harrison's tongue-in-cheek lyrics, McCartney plays some good, typical *Pepper*-era bass, underpinning the psychedelia flying around his head. For the title track of their next project, *Magical Mystery Tour*, he sticks to a more straightahead part, although there are moments to savour. It feels like he got the groove down and then jumped off with some little melodic figures to grab the attention here and there. What it doesn't feel like is a brand new style for a brand new album.

One of the best bass moments on the *Mystery Tour* record comes with 'Baby You're A Rich Man', recorded in May 1967. Right from the start, with a sequence of dead notes purely for percussive effect, we're into an unusual bass soundscape: now a dark, deep, mid-boosted tone and a galloping-horse rhythm. There's an engaging triad phrasing idea running off the vocal in the chorus from 1:15, and a remarkably quirky octave lick at 1:24 followed immediately by an intentional dissonance. You might think it's a mistake the first time you hear it, but no, he does it again in the second chorus, at 2:22.

See 'BABY YOU'RE A RICH MAN' opposite

Yet again, McCartney is making you listen. From *Pepper* he's retained his

interest in the different ways of making the note, rather than concentrating on the different sequences of notes. The Rickenbacker has released him to think more specifically about how it might sound when he does a particular thing. He knows he'll get a result on the Rick: if you lean into the note, you'll hear it.

George Martin wrote later: "Paul says his dad liked to play boogie-woogie on the piano, which is interesting when you look at Paul's own development into one of the world's great bass guitarists. In a boogie-woogie piano tune, the bassline, played by the left hand, produces a strong contrapuntal melody, rather than just a rhythmic thud. Paul's own bass guitar playing is of course the most melodic ever. He set a standard no one has ever reached. Sometimes he even composed songs around a bassline melody. Paul's bassline on 'Baby You're A Rich Man' is a good example of what he can do."[65]

McCartney himself was asked at the time to describe his bass sound. "I go for a very bassy but cutting sound. It's got to drive everything along. I like the separate notes to be distinguishable. Now that we lead more of a recording life I find that the piano and acoustic guitar are detracting a little from the bass, but I feel that it's always going to be my first love."[64]

Another highpoint in the otherwise largely dead time during the rest of 1967 came among the hoopla of the satellite-transmitted single 'All You Need Is Love', recorded in June. It follows 'Rich Man' in that McCartney establishes a groove and then creates fills off of and around that – but this one is even better. He is quite brilliant in his phrasing and control of the notes and the way in which he applies the bell-like tone of his Rickenbacker. Check that verse lick at 0:38:

See 'ALL YOU NEED IS LOVE' next page

Around the same time, they made 'It's All Too Much'. It's all too much of a psychedelic mess – but with a great bass moment as McCartney suddenly states the melody at 2:22. Towards the end of the year they recorded 'Hello Goodbye' as a new single A-side, and McCartney adds a typically meandering, melodic, Beatles-1967 bassline, with a lovely descending feature at the start, from 0:08:

See 'HELLO GOODBYE' opposite

Moving into the opening months of 1968, 'Lady Madonna', a single A-side, comes with a snarling bottom-end amid a souped-up walking bass. The verse groove is a standard pop-rock variation on walking bass where he plays pairs of the same note for a funkier feel, and it's worth a listen too for the way that he tracks the piano's left hand and adds a little embellishment coming off the guitar lick.

A few days later at Abbey Road came a real high-spot for McCartney's bass playing with 'Hey Bulldog', a gem that would be hidden away on the *Yellow Submarine* LP. If you haven't heard this song before, or simply overlooked it, prepare for a pleasant surprise. Here is a kinetic, busy, aggressive bassline. The bass guitar is again the lead melodic instrument, *Pepper*-style, but now with a funky influence and an improvisational feel:

See 'HEY BULLDOG' opposite

In May 1968 the group began work on their next LP, which would become *The Beatles*, or *The White Album* as it's better known. They would take until October to finish it. The result was a sprawling double-album with less complete character than *Pepper* but many passages of good bass work. And the great big organic bass growl on 'Dear Prudence' is a wonderful place to start.

It begins with McCartney's teasing single-note intro that suggests a spare bass part. How wrong can you be? What follows is a loping, brooding, hypnotic bassline that completely shifts the song's horizon. He allows Lennon, the song's composer, to sing more gracefully than he might otherwise have done, because the aggression is all there in the bass part underneath. McCartney makes the song sound more sophisticated than it is; in fact it has a relatively simple structure. But what a great sound as he squeezes out the top notes, drags them back down to the pedal root, and then does it all over again, with some beautifully subtle variations along the way. (See full transcription and analysis, page 142.)

The recording of *The White Album* was helped by the arrival of an 8-track tape recorder at Abbey Road and a suitable new mixing board. This meant there was less need to bounce material between recorders. Bouncing from 4-track to 4-track had always meant a loss in quality, despite the gain in space for more overdubs. 'Dear Prudence' was recorded in August 1968 and marked one of the group's first 8-track recordings, made at Trident studio in central London ('Hey Jude', started the previous month, had been the first, also at Trident). Their first 8-track recording at Abbey Road was 'While My Guitar Gently Weeps', coincidentally another *White Album* bass highlight.

■ 'All You Need Is Love'

Time: 0.38

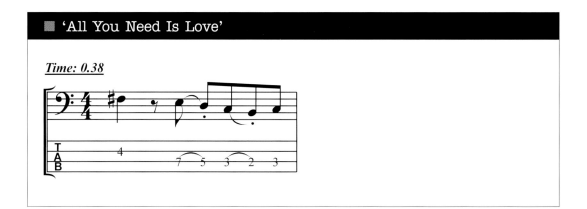

■ 'Hello Goodbye'

Time: 0.08

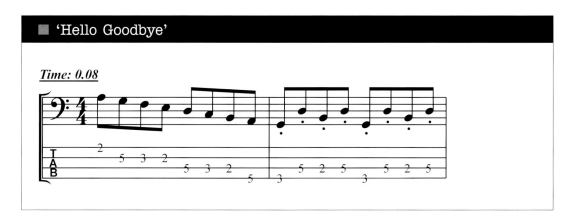

■ 'Hey Bulldog'

Time: 0.14

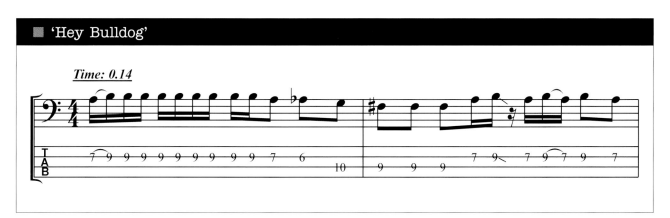

The bass is somewhat buried in the eight tracks of material on 'Gently Weeps'; you need to pan your stereo to the right to hear it properly. McCartney is crashing out double-stops with a lot of pick attack, going for power in the verses where he seems to consider his bass almost as a rhythm guitar. Listen to the guitar-solo section too, where there are plenty more double-stops going on underneath. There is a bass melody here, even if it is a simple one compared to some of his work on *Pepper*, and it's quite lyrical in places. Technically there is nothing complicated, but that's irrelevant, because musically this is very sophisticated.

A further bass high-spot comes with 'Everybody's Got Something To Hide Except Me And My Monkey'. For its bluesy, funky line McCartney leans again on James Jamerson and James Brown. It's another suitably aggressive line: he matches what he plays to Lennon's vocal and in the process provides the song with all the intensity it needs.

The single made during the *White Album* sessions was 'Hey Jude' / 'Revolution'. A slow version of Lennon's 'Revolution' recorded earlier was saved for the album, with McCartney's elegant complementary melodies at 0:49 and 1:53:

See 'REVOLUTION' below

The single version has another aggressive, driving bass part but lacks the grace of the album cut. On the A-side, however, McCartney doesn't need anything from the bass for his straightforward song, even though there is plenty of room, and he chooses to keep out of the way. Contrast this with the album's 'Sexy Sadie', a Lennon song where he takes a wandering melodic approach that he could easily have applied to 'Jude'.

'Cry Baby Cry' is another in the style of 'Sadie' as it too features one of those

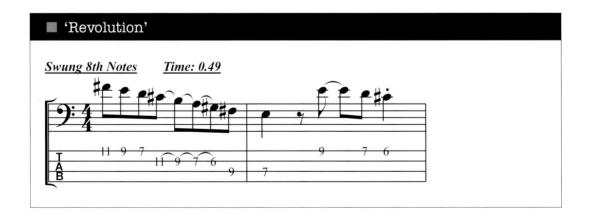

■ 'Revolution'

Swung 8th Notes   **Time: 0.49**

wandering melodic parts. The bass is rather low in the mix at first, but it wanders into view and meanders along in a pleasing way. Contrast that with something like 'Piggies', a very static if tidy bass job, or 'Why Don't We Do It In The Road' (although there is a lovely moment at 1:18 on this one that's impossible not to smile along with).

Harrison's 'Savoy Truffle' has rambling eighth-notes from the bass in the verse – and a heady lick at 1:20. George Martin took elements of the existing instrumentation, including the bassline, to score the later saxophone overdub, and at one point on the released version the horns almost double the bass. But there's no escaping that McCartney's playing feels retro in the way that he keeps within the octave, digging back a little to earlier playing. Perhaps it was simply nostalgia, given how far they'd come in just six years.

'Yer Blues' seems like more regression, despite the solid aggression and octave fills with an almost overdriven sound. But there's a worrying lack of direction evident. It's hard to imagine this is the group that a little over a year ago was making *Sgt Pepper*. One element of that album that does survive to the new record's bass playing is the sometimes brassy tuba-like tone and its appropriate role in the arrangement. 'The Continuing Story Of Bungalow Bill' and 'Happiness Is A Warm Gun' both have it (and McCartney uses some string-bends on 'Happiness', from 1:37, an unusual technique for him). 'I Will' has a peculiar 'vocalised' bass that gets even closer to the tuba impersonation, while 'Martha My Dear' again takes up the idea on bass guitar but adds some more along the way. And what an intelligent bassline it turns out to be when it does finally appear. Where the drive of the song pauses, McCartney takes the opportunity to add colour, a good example of how he often uses his bass to direct the listener through a tune.

McCartney generally used his Rickenbacker during the album sessions (and there is at least one photograph of him with a new left-handed Fender Jazz Bass), played through his now familiar Fender Bassman or the usual array of the newest Vox amps. Sometimes on *The White Album* the group adopted the simpler 'real' approach that they would take to its conclusion on *Let It Be* next year, and Lennon or Harrison would play a newly-acquired Fender VI six-string bass if McCartney was busy with keyboard or guitar work. McCartney explained the approach to an interviewer at the end of the *White Album* sessions: "On *Sgt Pepper* we had more instrumentation than we'd ever had, more orchestral stuff than we'd ever used before, so it was more of a production. But we didn't really want to go overboard like that this time, and we've tried to play more like a band this time – only using instruments when we had to, instead of just using them for the fun of it."[65]

Lennon plays the Fender VI bass part on 'Rocky Racoon', 'Back In The USSR', and probably 'Glass Onion', and it's probably Harrison on 'Birthday' and 'Honey Pie'. 'Helter Skelter' is sometimes credited to Lennon, sometimes to McCartney. Our guess is Lennon, but whoever it is, the aggressive bass playing is just part of the group's failure in their quest to make the song into a 'heavy' recording. They were apparently out of their heads, and the result is weak and embarrassing.

'Ob-La-Di Ob-La-Da' has a calypso-carnival feel attached to a nursery-rhyme of a song. "John plays piano, that's a great moment," says McCartney. "He came in, we were all rather sort of stale on it; I'd been rehearsing, and he was late. He came in: 'What we doing, what we doing?' I says 'Ob-La-Di Ob-La-Da' and instead of him picking up his guitar he went: [sings piano intro and opening bars], and we all went: 'Fucking hell!' Thought we were gonna hit the roof, and that became the total vibe of it all. And then I put the bass on after, and then double-tracked it with an acoustic guitar, which is a cool idea, an octave up from the bass, playing exactly the same. … It toughens it up."[66]

The White Album had not been an easy record to make, with plenty of tensions and tantrums among the group. (Engineer Geoff Emerick stopped working with them during these sessions, tired of their bickering.) McCartney's idea for the next project was to develop the original *White Album* notion: a simpler, back-to-basics approach. The group would 'get back' to the way they used to work: no overdubs, just live takes. It must have seemed like a good idea at the time.

Get Back, as it was first called, was fraught with problems, many of which have been dealt with at (great) length elsewhere and do not directly concern us here. The recordings absorbed the group between January and May 1969. What we ended up with was an album eventually issued in 1970 as *Let It Be*, produced by Phil Spector, and a revised version released in 2003 as *Let It Be … Naked*.

The idea at the start of 1969 was that the new record would present only what the four members (sometimes plus keyboardist Billy Preston) could play live, captured by engineer-producer Glyn Johns. But the version released in 1970 – actually the last Beatles album to come out, because it was delayed until after *Abbey Road* – was taken well beyond that when Spector was brought in. He added orchestral instruments and choral vocals to some of the songs. The recent *Naked*

version, put together after prompting by McCartney, reflects the original intention and is closer to the no-overdubs idea.

The *Naked* engineers mostly used the same takes as the Johns and Spector versions, with some exceptions, all of which they cleaned up and remastered, notably removing the orchestrations that Spector had added. (The only take changed completely for *Naked* is 'The Long And Winding Road'; the compilers opted for the last one recorded, which they felt was a stronger performance and had the benefit of the latest version of the lyrics.) *Naked* as a whole sounds better than the original *Let It Be*. There's also an entertaining bonus disc of chat and song fragments assembled by Kevin Howlett, who bravely listened to 80 hours of *Get Back/Let It Be* tapes. "I had expected to hear the kind of disagreements and arguing we've all heard about," said Howlett. "Instead I heard the band members actually having a good time. By the end they were in fact quite excited about what they were doing."[67]

Howlett's point is a good one. *Let It Be* does have the reputation of a sloppy jam album, but even a brief listen will tell you that there is a good deal of arranged material here. And anyway, why would a group so used to that approach suddenly stop? They might think they had, but 'Don't Let Me Down' is a good example that shows otherwise. This song has been carefully worked out – even if the performance has a raw edge to it and some of the instruments are, shall we say, not quite in tune. There's even a slick unison bass/guitar line on the bridge, starting at 1:18, something that the group had rarely indulged in until now:

See 'DON'T LET ME DOWN' next page

There's more Fender six-string bass on some of the *Let It Be* songs, following on from its use on *The White Album* and the idea now that everything had to be played live. If McCartney was on keyboards or guitar, then Lennon or Harrison would pick up the VI. This is what happens on 'Two Of Us' (Harrison), and 'Let It Be' and 'The Long And Winding Road' (Lennon). On 'For You Blue' there is no bass at all, thus providing your special play-along-with-The-Beatles 12-bar opportunity.

What does that leave for McCartney and his bass? 'Dig A Pony' has the group evidently enjoying themselves, wallowing in some more guitar/bass unisons. Have a listen to the fine intro:

See 'DIG A PONY' next page

McCartney's playing on the song has something of a *White Album* vibe: tidy, and with good ideas. 'I've Got A Feeling' characterises the best of the basic approach of

and in the end...

'Don't Let Me Down'

Time: 1.18

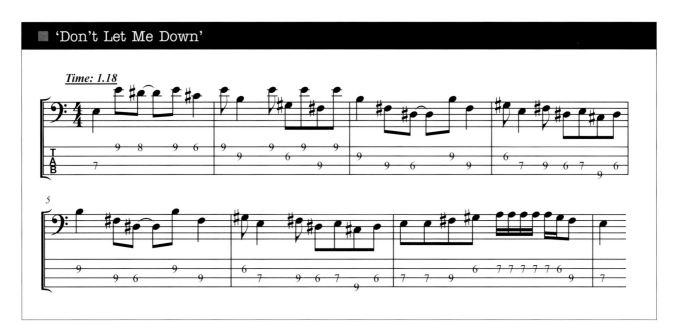

'Dig A Pony'

Swung 1/8th Notes

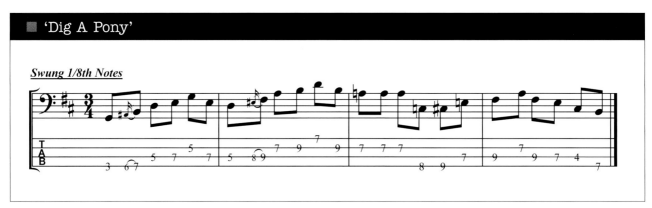

'I've Got A Feeling'

Time: 2.05

the record. He lays down a straightforward, effective ostinato octave drone for the verse, with a typical fill at 0:36 and a slight expansion under John Lennon's vocals at 2:05:

See 'I'VE GOT A FEELING' opposite

For a good deal of the studio work and the famous rooftop 'concert' filmed for the accompanying *Let It Be* movie, McCartney played his old Hofner again, usually through a new 'silverface' Fender Bassman rig. "Because the Hofner's so light," he recalls, "you play it a bit like a guitar. All that sort of high trilling stuff I used to do I think was because of the Hofner. When I play a heavier bass ... it sits me down a bit and I play just bass. But I noticed in the *Let It Be* film I play it right up there in 'Get Back' or something, and I think it was because it was such a light little guitar that it led you to play anywhere on it. Really, it led you to be a bit freer."[68] 'Get Back', on the roof or down in the studio, is a simple drone with octaves and minor sevenths.

The lengthy recordings and filming for *Get Back/Let It Be* tested the patience of everyone involved, despite the musical results. McCartney's next scheme – and, as it turned out, The Beatles' last – was a proper studio album, with George Martin and Geoff Emerick back with them at Abbey Road, which provided the title. It was recorded primarily in July and August 1969, although some songs had been started earlier.

Martin has said that there were fewer tensions during the recording of *Abbey Road* than *Let It Be*. "I thought I would never work with them again," he remembered later. "I thought, what a shame to go out that way. So I was quite surprised when Paul rang me up and said: 'We're going to make another record; would you like to produce it?' And my immediate answer was: 'Only if you let me produce it the way we used to.' And he said to me: 'We want to do that.' And I said: 'John included?' He said: 'Yes, honestly.' So I said: 'If you really want to do that, let's do it and get together again.' And it was a very happy record. I guess it was happy because everybody knew it was going to be the last."[69]

Certainly *Abbey Road* is in marked sonic contrast to *Let It Be*. True to McCartney's word, The Beatles were a studio group again, making full use of the technology at their disposal. *Abbey Road* turned out to be their most 'produced' record ever. The story goes that Lennon was keen to have self-contained songs as usual, hence the opening side of the original vinyl, while it was McCartney who put together the 'suite' of continuous work on side two, helped with its compilation by

George Martin. They even used one of those new-fangled synthesiser things.

Harrison's 'Old Brown Shoe' was recorded early in the new sessions and ended up as the B-side to 'The Ballad Of John And Yoko'. Pan your stereo to the left for 'Shoe' and you'll hear some fine bass playing that's otherwise rather buried. Even if these are mainly blues ideas, they're cleanly executed at a fierce tempo. And check these sequences:

See 'OLD BROWN SHOE' opposite

Abbey Road has some glittering bass highlights, with McCartney using his Rickenbacker through the new Fender Bassman amp. 'Something' is in our view the best piece of bass playing he's ever committed to record. There, we've said it. It's awesome: always musical and never merely technical. Any discussion of the all-time greatest bass playing on a pop ballad should include this remarkable gem.

McCartney creates melodies just as strong, memorable, and effective as Harrison's vocal, and he breathes life into his bassline in various ways: first with his subtle use of dynamics, for example in the opening bar of each verse, where he virtually crescendos the octave Cs in little over half a beat (first heard at 0:06); with the slides between notes, for example at 0:30, which help the lazy, lyrical vibe; and then with his use of subtle vibrato, for example in the second bar of the first verse (0:09) and under the guitar solo (2:01), which adds a little spice where he allows the bassline to settle briefly.

The tone of McCartney's Rickenbacker is also a vital element: the bottom end is rubbery yet full of fundamentals, and there's just enough pick attack for definition. Here is a telling combination of an understanding engineer and a player who knows more than a bit about tone. The bass on 'Something' is, quite simply, a joy to listen to.

'Come Together' has a fabulous world-class groove. At its heart is a basic, effective bass riff, but it marks the pinnacle of McCartney's playing in his extended-range style. He hits the root (D), reaches out for the fifth (A), slides to the minor seventh (C), and then grabs the minor third above (F). Here's the groove:

See 'COME TOGETHER' first bar opposite

At 1:26 he comes up with one of a number of tasty variations:

See 'COME TOGETHER' second bar opposite

He's back to the tuba impersonations on *Abbey Road*. On 'Maxwell's Silver Hammer' McCartney is remarkably effective and open, and this too marks the pinnacle of this particular style. It's almost as if he's drawing together some of his

■ 'Old Brown Shoe'

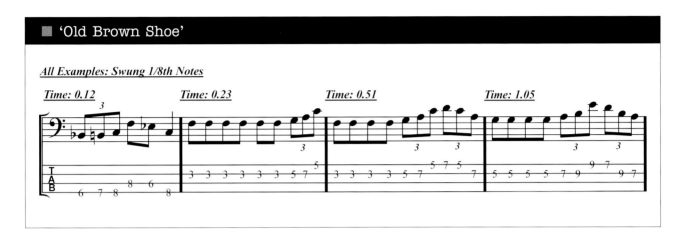

■ 'Come Together'

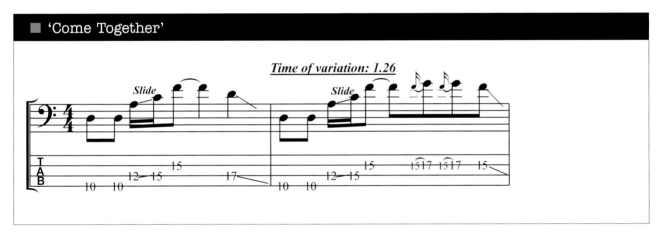

best styles for display on this album as some kind of final statement. For 'Maxwell', just sit back, ignore the lightweight song, and listen to an exuberant bass player enjoying himself. Keep an ear open especially for some stupendous spontaneous runs at 0:42 and 1:41:

See 'MAXWELL'S SILVER HAMMER' next page

There's more mock tuba when he gets to 'Octopus's Garden'. Despite the silliness of the song, he's in a rockier, more joyful mood, with one of a number of neat runs at 0:20 and a slippery octave fill at 1:33, and he opens out effectively underneath the solo. The earlier take two preserved on 1996's *Anthology 3* also has some lively moments worth a listen.

Highlighted amid the aggressive but not excessive bass part of 'I Want You' are some spectacular rhythmic glissandos, at 2:15, 4:05, 4:55, and 5:00, and some luscious bass breaks, at 0:56-1:02 and 1:47-1:53:

and in the end...

HERE COMES THE SUN

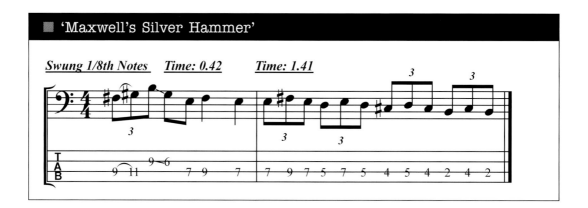

See 'I WANT YOU' first bar above

and at 3:08-3:14 and 4:27-4:33:

See 'I WANT YOU' second bar above

It's also notable the way McCartney follows Lennon's vocal with a spiky lick or simple accentuation to fill the gaps – but not always.

On Harrison's strong tune 'Here Comes The Sun' we have classic McCartney playing-for-the-song, using the bass to guide the listener through. Check the fill at 1:06; the way he focuses the melody on the bridge, from 1:30; and the simple pedal-note building of tension from 2:04 to 2:11. 'Because' is a perfect example of beautiful simplicity, where McCartney elects to stay out of the way while still providing solid rhythmic support. On 'Oh Darling' he's back to the tuba tone, with phrasing that matches the aggressive vocal, although what he plays more or less abides by the rules of the blues.

Abbey Road's 'suite' of songs originally took up side two of the vinyl.

McCartney's ability to leave space is highlighted on the opening section of the first song, 'You Never Give Me Your Money'. When the band kicks in he walks back to his roots, and later takes the opportunity to hit us with a few octave fills, first heard at 3:07 (and in hyperdrive at 3:28). In 'Sun King' too the bass is all about space and dynamics, and that pedal octave on the chord change – heard right from the front of the track – is an interesting device, while 'Mean Mr Mustard' gives McCartney the opportunity to be appropriately spiteful with his fuzz bass.

The classiest bass playing in the suite can be heard during 'She Came In Through The Bathroom Window' where McCartney adopts a fundamentally quarter-note walking bass approach, allowing the drums to be expressive, and then gets funkier from the second verse ("She said she'd always been a dancer..."). Next comes 'Golden Slumbers', where he orchestrates his line, tailoring the phrasing just so, while 'Carry That Weight' is about playing a part to drive the song along and then adding ornamentation in the right places.

'The End' features the famous three-way guitar duel, with McCartney, Harrison, and Lennon blasting away – two bars each, three times around – as McCartney really does get back to his original role as guitarist in The Beatles. Oddly, the final 30 seconds or so (1:29 to 2:01), after the piano break, has no bass at all. Thus the last proper track on The Beatles' last proper album has no final goodbye from McCartney and his bass. Given the heavy message of the rest of this song and its position on the album, is he trying to tell us something?

We're going to end here as The Beatles themselves end, even though McCartney has of course continued his own career very successfully. He says: "Ringo and I used to talk about it – and we still do occasionally – that our real dream is to be in the back of a very dark club, with shades on, playing bass and drums, and having about three or four other people doing the show. And we just want to be not noticed and just play music, man."[70]

John Lennon had this to say about McCartney the bassman: "Paul's bass playing is underrated. Paul was one of the most innovative bass players ever. And half the stuff that is going on now is directly ripped off from his Beatles period."[71] Lennon was absolutely right. It's Paul McCartney's playing in The Beatles that sets him apart as a world-class bassist – which is precisely what we've aimed to show in this book. As McCartney himself says: "Number one, The Beatles were the best band in the world. It's difficult to follow that. It's like following God. Very difficult, unless you're Buddha."[72]

Getting to grips with a Beatle bassline

transcriptions and analyses

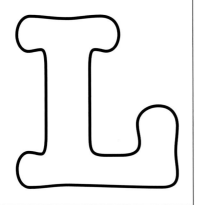

ike most working musicians, Paul McCartney often can't remember what he did on certain records. After all, it's not "20 years ago today" but around 40 years since The Beatles recorded their songs. As McCartney himself has told us, he and his group would try anything in the way of unusual instruments or unusual ways of playing an instrument, just to see what they sounded like or what difference they made. Given all that, how can we expect him to remember the details of one three-hour period on one day when he never kept a note of what he did? He didn't have the luxury of a computer on which to save his ideas and he couldn't read or write standard notation.

The Beatles didn't write anything with one eye on posterity. They had enquiring minds, highly fertile imaginations, and a producer in George Martin who was attuned and dedicated to realising their creative flights of fancy, however bizarre. From around 1966 they enjoyed completely unfettered studio access. This was a privilege that benefited other great innovators of the period, including bassists James Jamerson and Donald 'Duck' Dunn. Those two spent so much time in the Motown and Stax-Volt studios that they probably began to forget what the outside world looked like. But just listen to the results of their imprisonment. The same is true of McCartney and his group.

Great exponents of an art seldom use their brilliance simply in pursuit of some higher concept. They do it because they love it. It's in their blood and at the core of their being. They simply have to. McCartney didn't fear explanation but he wasn't particularly interested in it. There's a degree of the "if I know how I do it maybe I won't be able to any more" attitude. But if you're coming up with songs and records that consistently sell in millions and you know you're creating good music, why concern yourself?

Suppose 'Please Please Me' had been their only hit in five years. It's hard to imagine The Beatles (or any other group for that matter) sitting around a table and saying: "OK, so what made that song so good and how can we reproduce that magic?" McCartney in particular and The Beatles in general never had to do that, because the magic evolved in a way that always had mass appeal. The lesson is simple: just follow your instincts.

Studying how and why a good player made certain musical decisions adds to our musical knowledge in the same way as learning the major scale. The musical mind works by simmering away for years: everything a player hears is potentially an influence.

So, here are nine Beatles tracks with bass transcription and a detailed analysis for each song. This is the close-listening part of the book where we examine the detail of McCartney's style and genius.

A note of caution: don't turn into a clone. There is no point in sounding exactly like another musician. It is not creative – even if there is a tribute band down the street looking for a 'Paul'. To model yourself entirely on one other musician is short-sighted, unambitious, and really quite sad. Learn what you can, steal any number of licks, even buy a violin bass, but be yourself. Then in 40 years it might be your name on the front cover of a book like this.

Drive My Car

verse 1 "Ask ..."

chorus 1 "Baby ..."

verse 2 "I told ..."

chorus 2 "Baby ..."

guitar solo

chorus 3 "Baby ..."

verse 3 "I told ..."

chorus 4 "Baby ..."

outro

Recorded Oct 13th 1965
Released on *Rubber Soul*,
Dec 3rd 1965 (UK),
Dec 6th 1965 (US)

Words and Music by John Lennon and
Paul McCartney
Copyright © 1965 Sony/ATV Songs LLC
Copyright Renewed
This arrangement Copyright © 2006
Sony/ATV Songs LLC
All Rights Administered by Sony/ATV
Music Publishing, 8 Music Square West,
Nashville, TN 37203, USA
International Copyright Secured
All Rights Reserved

'**D**rive My Car' is clearly a McCartney composition – he dominates the lead vocal – but Lennon's influence looms large in this mid-period Beatles classic: the undercurrent of cynicism, the lyrical double entendres, and the moody power in the chorus. McCartney's bass playing helps to emphasise all this while still allowing the song to breathe freely.

His bass in the verses hints at taking the listener for a ride, though it's hardly seat-of-the-pants stuff: only half the bar has any movement, taking the form of a cool unison with Harrison's grating, single-note rhythm part. McCartney intelligently throws in a funky sixteenth-note pick-up every second bar (for example bar 4 at 0:08) to head off any feeling of stagnation, and at the end of each verse there's a build up of tension as his bass part more or less marks time for a bar and a half before hitting us with another wicked unison lick (for example bar 10 at 0:20), although this time it's flat-out funky.

The small changes that McCartney makes to his verse part involve him removing rather than adding notes (for example in verse two, bar 20, at 0:39). The really cool variation comes under Harrison's first solo where McCartney adds a bluesy grace-note feel to the second half of the D bar (F to F-sharp, for example bar 59 at 1:09) and fills out the G riff with a wickedly funky lick over the fourth beat (for example bar 36 at 1:11).

He stays within a fairly limited melodic range in the verse, never going above a fifth (D to A, G to D) until the last bar. 'Drive My Car' is a well-organised, repetitive affair and isn't supposed to sound like it wanders in the way that 'You Won't See Me' or the highly improvisational 'Rain' do.

The chorus is a pounding, quarter-note juggernaut rampaging along until another brooding unison (bar 16 at 0:30) heralds a two-bar resolution, as if the lights are about to go red: this is, quite simply, McCartney demonstrating mastery of a theme. This part of the groove is all about aggressive forward motion so root notes are the order of the day, excepting the use of a nifty A to guide the B minor chord to G (for example bar 11 at 0:22) and vice versa (for example bar 12 at 0:24). There are a few funky kicks, especially the first bar of the third chorus (bar 59 at 1:55), but mostly the requirement is to emphasise the sheer power that underpins proceedings.

As if feeling that he's fulfilled his brief, McCartney discards the shackles of repetition and finally allows himself to rock out over the climactic guitar solo, discarding the basic verse groove to chug away on solid eighth-notes, while more or less keeping to the same note choices (for example bar 69 at 2:14). Listen to the effect when he staccatos them at 2:19 (bar 72) and 2:21 (bar 74): now that's some serious attitude.

This song goes through a couple of related keys. Verses sit firmly in D, but given Lennon's influence on the chorus it's not surprising that it moves squarely into the related key of B minor. The only unusual chord comes over the unison in bar six of the chorus (for example chorus 1, at 0:30) where instead of the E minor chord expected in the key of D they substitute E major, which leads more strongly to A and provides some fleeting tension.

All in all, there's a feeling of disciplined joy here. McCartney's not striving to be creative: he's after the groove-power he knows he can get by staying in a fairly low register. The combination of thrust and melody turns this wicked little morsel into a template for many a rock/funk bassline to follow.

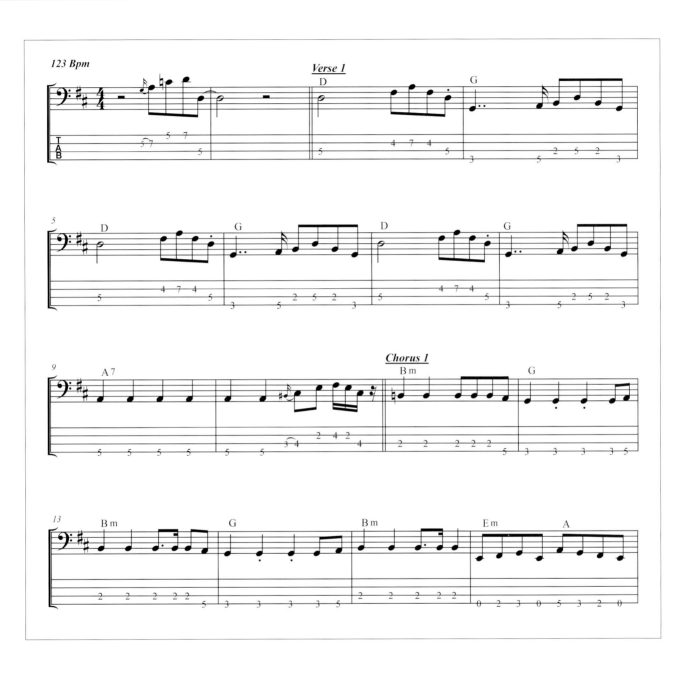

drive my car

drive my car

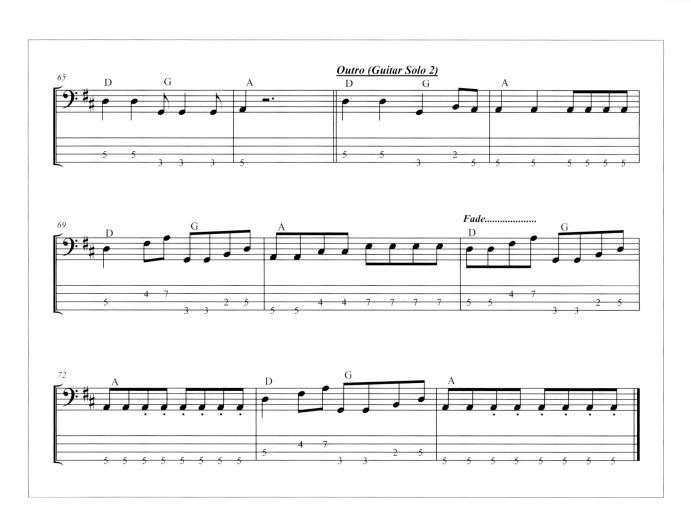

In My Life

verse 1 "There ..."

chorus 1 "All ..."

verse 2 "But ..."

chorus 2 "Though ..."

piano solo

chorus 3 "Though ..."

coda

Recorded Oct 18th 1965,
plus Oct 22nd (piano solo
overdub)
Released on *Rubber Soul*,
Dec 3rd 1965 (UK),
Dec 6th 1965 (US)

This is a beautiful, reflective Lennon ballad and McCartney, totally in tune with the mood of the song, delivers a piece of world class groove playing, with Ringo in close attendance. The feel is perfect and the strong emotional impact of this technically simple part finds McCartney matching Lennon's vocal intensity virtually note for note on the trusty Hofner.

Right from the introduction, with its subtle quarter-note footsteps and staccato semi-unison (bar 1 at 0:02), you know that McCartney will not waste a note. The verse opens solidly, supportively, and uneventfully, but the second bar is a wake-up call. The dissonant G (bar 6 at 0:13) is just gorgeous and as near as we'll ever get to Pablo Picasso on bass, such is the feeling of drama it creates in emphasising the retrospective element of Lennon's lyric. The remainder of the verse cycle is simple and tasteful, with staccato phrasing (again bar 6 at 0:13) and plenty of space (bar 7 at 0:15) helping us to fully absorb the mood.

One notable but not particularly audible ornamentation is the double-stop in bar 11 (0:24, comprising the notes D and A), but when he gets to the chorus McCartney uses this far more effectively. In the two bars where the forward motion pauses briefly (13 and 14 from 0:28 to 0:32) he plays a couple of double-stops, an F-sharp/C sharp followed by a D/A. The effect is as surprising and perfect as that dissonant G.

There's a smooth tone to these double-stops (and to the whole line in general) that suggests McCartney may have used his fingers or even the side of his thumb, not his usual pick. Whatever the playing technique he chose, it produces a wonderfully even response, filling acres of space without clutter and increasing the feeling of wistful melancholy. As Lennon picks up the intensity of the vocal, McCartney tracks him with two bars of rumbling eighth-notes (15 and 16 from 0:33 to 0:37) before the sequence repeats itself and the introduction is restated. The second chorus is a fraction busier than the first (bar 31, at 1:10) but McCartney has the good taste to peg himself back in the third: as the song begins to die away, so does the bass part.

'In My Life' resides in the key of A and, although it moves around a little, McCartney refrains from adding much in the way of melodic colour. He implies a G major chord in bar 6 (0:13) by almost inaudibly sneaking in a B and a D (the other two notes of the triad). Playing a double-stop of root and fifth (D and A on this occasion) when D minor substitutes D major in bar 25 (0:57) doesn't add any colour in the way that the third of the chord (F) would have. The eighth-note line under the chorus G major chord (in bar 15 at 0:33) is also a simple, solid root-note affair, although a tasty G-sharp pops up to lead us back to A in the third chorus (from bar 49 into 50 at 1:54).

Other than the ornamentations already mentioned, McCartney employs slides, with the one leading from the first verse to the chorus (bar 12, at 0:27) sounding almost like an intake of breath, but surprisingly few grace notes, though there's a nice one at the start of the eighth-note cluster in bar 16 at 0:35. There are some sneaky sixteenth-note pick-ups if you listen carefully, mostly purely rhythmic but no less classy for it, such as bar 19 (0:43) where he seems to be trying to match Harrison's rhythmic arpeggiation. In the third chorus right at the end of bar 48 (1:51) a neat little lick hustles you into bar 49, where McCartney abandons the simple eighth-note approach, introducing a tad more space into the first half of the bar before subtly funking-up the third beat (1:54).

In truth, what McCartney plays on this song is much less important than how he plays it – and the 'how' is a feast of pure, unadulterated feel. The way he tracks the dynamic of Lennon's vocal throughout the song is a simple lesson in beautifully effective groove playing.

in my life

in my life

The Word

chorus 1 "Say ..."

verse 1 "In ..."

chorus 2 "Spread ..."

verse 2 "Everywhere ..."

chorus 3 "Say ..."

verse 3 "Now ..."

chorus 4 "Give ..."

organ solo 1

chorus 5 "Say ..."

organ solo 2

Recorded Nov 10th 1965
Released on *Rubber Soul*,
Dec 3rd 1965 (UK),
Dec 6th 1965 (US)

Only John Lennon could have written a song around the word 'love' and have it come out as a spiteful, aggressive tirade against his own naivety and emotional failings. Thankfully, he seems to reach a state of understanding and redemption before it's all over. McCartney gleefully grabs the opportunity to dig in, and the result is a seriously kicking, spiky funk-rock bass monster.

'The Word' is essentially in the key of D but uses as the foundation of the harmony the dominant seventh chord (a major triad with a minor seventh, here D-F#-A-C). This tells us that it's the bluesy version, and the intrinsically tense sound provides Lennon with the perfect environment for his aggressive pontificating.

Underneath, McCartney's chorus bassline is a rhythmically identical call-and-response affair, diving down to A from D via C (for example bar 2 at 0:02) and then scampering back up again using cool chromatic steps (C to C-sharp: for example bar 2, at 0:03). The overall vibe of this section is based on jerky, staccato, almost locked-up note lengths – and is so carefully controlled that when McCartney allows himself the luxury of sustain it has a big impact on the groove, like a massive intake of breath. McCartney will occasionally relax his tight control of note lengths, such as the full quarter-note towards the end of the first verse (bar 14, at 0:25) and the generous half-bar legato offering towards the end of the third chorus (in bar 43, at 1:21). These provide some relief, but are still rarities.

McCartney goes for a rhythmically simplified line in the final chorus, this time allowing the notes in the first half of each bar to sing out before reverting to tighter note-length control in the second half (for example bar 70, at 2:14). It's remarkable how less busy the part feels after the removal of only one sixteenth-note – have a listen to bars 57 (1:49) and 72 (2:18) for an effective comparison. Equally effective is the way that McCartney outlines the sus4-to-major chord change just before the painfully short verses (for example bar 28 into 29, from 0:52 to 0:55). Sure, it's a little kitsch – but it's hard to imagine how fewer or more notes could have worked better at this point.

When McCartney does reach the verse he drives the groove in the simplest yet most effective manner: with quarter-notes. Not only that, but he restricts himself to the root of each chord (for example bars 16 to 20, from 0:28 to 0:37). There's one real nugget of a lick that McCartney uses to mark the transition from verse to chorus: the first is in bar 19 (at 0:36); there's a laidback variation in bar 51 (1:38);

and the busiest version comes in bar 67 (2:09). It's a classic case of McCartney intelligently flagging-up a section change – and it just happens to restate the funk, too.

You'd think that McCartney would be satisfied with his fiery funk work-out in the chorus. But this is, after all, a Lennon composition and McCartney is still intent on making the maximum impact on the song (within reason) through his contribution on bass. To this end he pulls two wonderful blues-scale fills out of his hat. The real joy here is that while the first time (bar 39, at 1:14) helps the change from D7 to G7, the second time (bar 73, at 2:21) the chords are moving in the opposite direction. Best of all, McCartney never alters the phrasing of the lick, although it is one he'll come back to in a couple of notable compositions (both of which follow shortly: 'Rain' and 'Taxman').

McCartney's groove on 'The Word' marks a high point in pop bass playing and as such is the first proof on a recording of his serious technical ability on the instrument. There's an arrogant self-confidence in the execution that has a wholly positive effect on the song. That McCartney is beginning to sound like he's having a lot of fun is refreshing, especially amid such high quality musical ideas.

the word

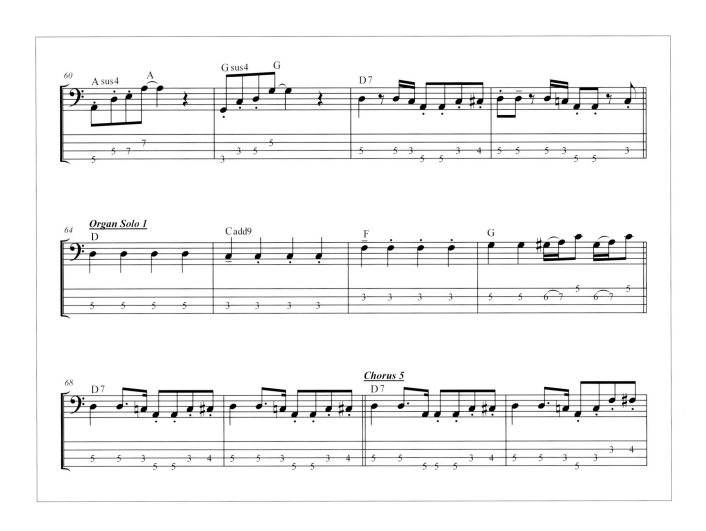

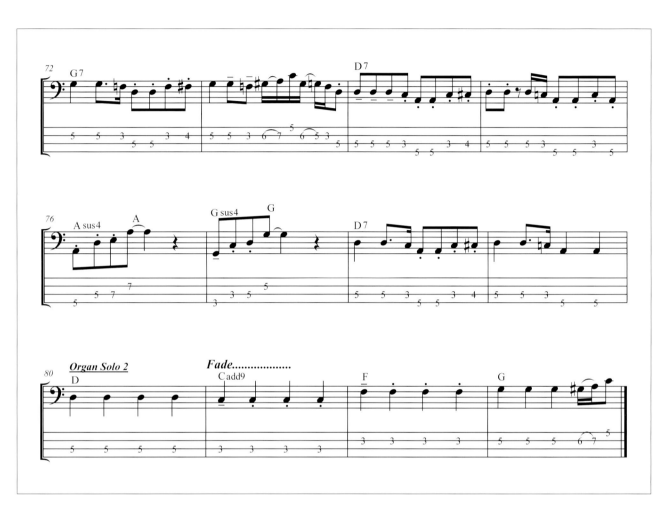

You Won't See Me

verse 1 "When ..."

verse 2 "I don't ..."

bridge 1 "Time ..."

verse 3 "Though ..."

bridge 2 "Time ..."

verse 4 "Though ..."

outro

Recorded Nov 11th 1965
Released on *Rubber Soul*,
Dec 3rd 1965 (UK),
Dec 6th 1965 (US)

This classic piece of McCartney-penned pop from 1965 conveniently acts as a bridge between the band's early and later periods, its springy, melodic eighth-note pop feel married to an underlying (albeit sporadic) sixteenth-note funkiness.

It's also a song of contrasts, where the carefree exuberance of the verse singularly fails to match the more contemplative mood and message of the vocal on top. The wandering melodic nature of the bass in the verses is answered astutely by the more solid and static bridges, the second of which hints at the generally funkier attitude that McCartney would soon pursue. Throw in the fact that he goes for a fairly pushy feel (especially in the verse) and this is a fantastic example of a supportive yet free-flowing McCartney groove. He's almost nonchalant in the way he controls the drive and dynamics of this song.

The impression is that for the verses he has an almost endless variety of note choices, but in fact the first half of almost every bar is a repetition, using the staple of root, third, and fifth (A-C#-E in the case of A major, for example bar 3 at 0:04), firm evidence of the unbreakable ties with his rock'n'roll-blues roots. He introduces a nice selection of variations over beats two and three that keep you guessing.

The song is essentially in the key of A, but there are some altered chords dictated purely by the requirements of the vocal melody. McCartney deals with the most frequent one (B major replacing B minor) by playing D-sharp instead of the key-appropriate D (for example in bar 4 at 0:07). But he ducks the issue of D minor temporarily replacing D major until the third verse, finally using an F there within the standard triadic pattern in the first half of the bar (see bar 57, at 1:55).

Check out the opening bar of verse three (1:34). The single quarter-note on the first beat sounds like a mistake (although there's not a 'wrong' note in sight), and might well have been, but McCartney uses the same idea, albeit for two beats instead of one, at the start of the last verse (bar 73 at 2:28). As the saying goes: it's no longer a mistake if you do it twice.

The execution of this part involves regular grace notes, which really make it speak. By clipping some of the note lengths (staccato) he creates both a feeling of space (when there really isn't any) and injects just a hint of classy funk – for example at 0:10 and 1:18. The way McCartney connects certain chord changes by simply sliding up or down the same string (for example at 1:30) lends a lazy air to proceedings, and the double-stop towards the end of the first verse (at 0:25), while probably a mistake, is simply ultra cool.

Overall, he's having a lot of fun. The odd glitch here and there (like the patently wrong note at the start of the first bridge, 1:18) neither bothers nor fazes him. This is classic pop bass playing with a highly improvisatory edge and represents the absolute pinnacle of McCartney's style during his early Beatles period.

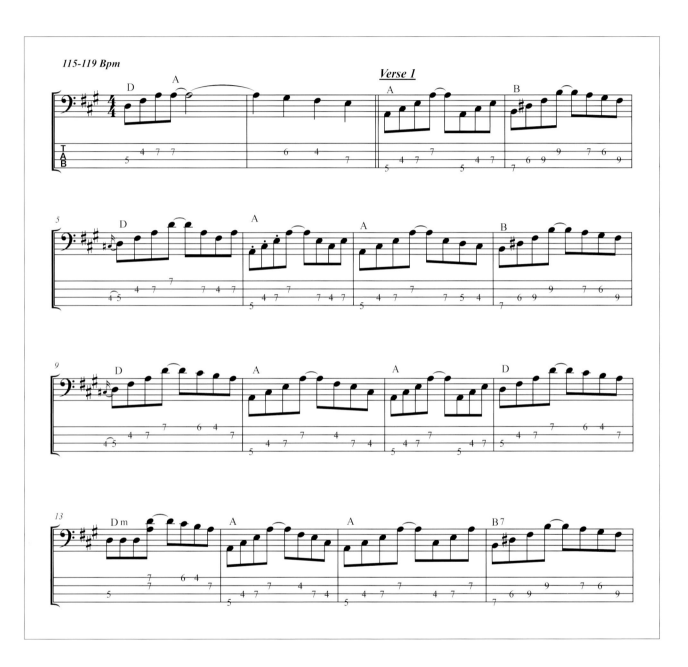

you won't see me

you won't see me

you won't see me

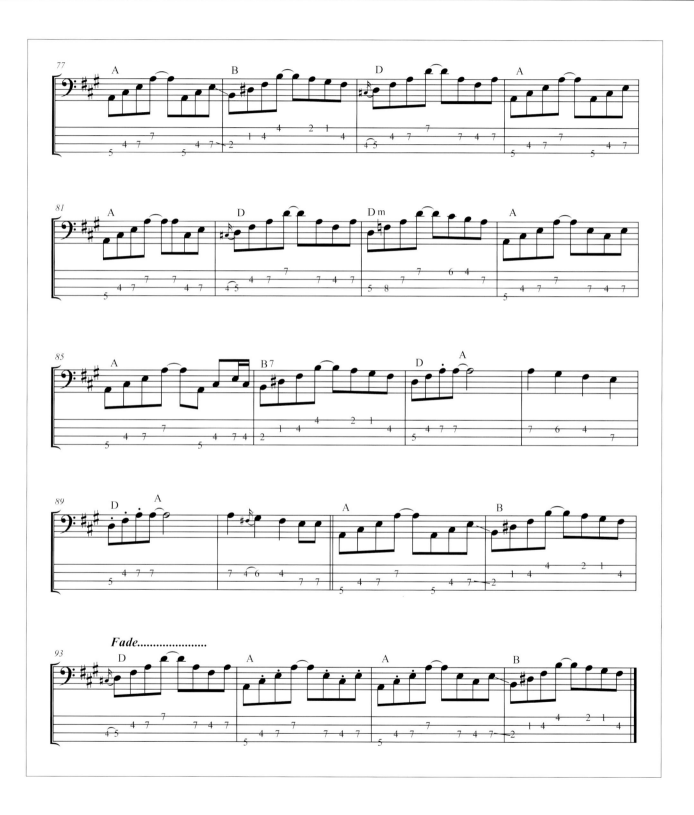

Rain

verse 1 "If ..."

verse 2 "When ..."

bridge 1 "Rain..."

verse 3 "I can ..."

bridge 2 "Rain..."

verse 4 "Can ..."

outro

Recorded Apr 14th 1966,
plus Apr 16th (overdubs,
probably including bass)
Released as B-side on
'Paperback Writer' single,
May 30th 1966 (US),
Jun 10th 1966 (UK)

'Rain' is a wonderful piece of Lennon psychedelia about one of his favourite pastimes of this period – taking LSD. McCartney, meanwhile, plays way up the neck of his Rickenbacker and seldom strays, an intransigence that lends an unstoppable insistence to this funk tour de force. It marks one of the first instances where McCartney is given extra space and simply rejoices in it.

It's interesting that he turns in such an astonishing piece of playing on a song that, although it has obvious Eastern influences in the vocal and the droning guitar parts, is fundamentally built on what can best be described as simple blues harmony: chords I (G), IV (C), and V (D), albeit in their simplest (triadic) form. OK, so there is a little drift into sus4 territory, but that harmonic vibe never dominates.

Why is he playing in such a high register? McCartney too was after a drone effect and he realised that if he played too low for too long, then an already bassy recording could become a dirge. He's thinking in terms of both rhythm and 'lead bass' and so he chooses the area of the neck around the tenth fret that he correctly perceives will give him clarity for melody without rendering his sound too thin for groove. He's been playing the Rickenbacker for almost a year by now and knows how to get the sound he wants from it.

The relative featurelessness of the harmony certainly doesn't restrict McCartney's ideas. Remember, this is a bass player whose level of self-belief is at an all-time high. It's as if he's saying: "Well, John, if you're gonna give me the space to show off, that's what I'll do!" Right from the opening bar (0:01) it's a funk party for thrill-seekers only, but one which features a surprisingly limited use of range. Why surprising? Because there are plenty of opportunities all over the song for expansive playing and McCartney is definitely in the mood to go for it. We'd argue (somewhat bizarrely given the nature of the part) that it's also a highly disciplined piece of playing.

For the G chord, the body of McCartney's line is root with answering octave, rapidly followed by a cool hammer-on (C to D, for example bar 10 at 0:20). Most of the time he uses F to cap it all off, the minor seventh against G, for a bluesy edge (bar four at 0:08), but occasionally for variation he slips in another high G (for example bar 41 at 1:27). For the C and D chords, McCartney sticks mainly to the root note, other than when the song rests on C for two bars (for example 11 and

12, from 0:21 to 0:25) where he throws in some spicey chromatic runs (for example bar 11 at 0:22).

There are lots of other licks worth mentioning, especially the reappearance of blues-scale varieties. Just as in 'The Word', McCartney uses them in two different ways. First, in bars 16 (0:32) and 18 (0:37), where the song is moving from the C to D chords; second, in bar 37 (1:17, right at the start of a verse for maximum impact!), as the chords move from G to C. There are other fine variations to enjoy, such as the country guitar lick in bar 57 (2:03) and its funkier cousin two bars later (2:08). How about that machine-gun hammer-on (bar 61 at 2:12)? Nobody else could have made that sound as cool as McCartney! The whole final vamp section from the breakdown (bars 67 to 82, from 2:25 until the track has faded) is a study in subtle variation on a theme. It's so much fun to listen to.

Our old friend the grace note is a regular guest at this bassline party, whether in the verse (for example bar 38 at 1:19) where it increases the lazy, vocal element of McCartney's phrasing, or in the first bridge (for example bar 25 to 28, from 0:50 to 0:59) where it bolsters the trance-like nature of McCartney's pedal-note idea. The sheer bravery in repeating this simple lick so many times should be loudly applauded. It builds up massive tension and anticipation, too, and is evidence of McCartney's realisation that he has power over the flow of the song.

This is easily one of McCartney's best basslines, and not solely for the technique involved. The feel is excellent, with a lazy, funky edge and a tone that's perfect in the context. The way he maximises his ideas in a restricted range and the volume and quality of the variations on offer help to make this something very special indeed.

De-Tune E-string to D

Verse 1

Verse 2

rain

rain

Taxman

verse 1 "Let ..."

chorus 1 "Cos ..."

verse 2 "Should ..."

chorus 2 "Cos ..."

bridge "If ..."

guitar solo 1

chorus 3 "Cos ..."

verse 3 "Don't ..."

chorus 4 "Cos ..."

verse 4 "Now ..."

chorus 5 "Cos ..."

guitar solo 2

Recorded Apr 21st 1966,
plus Apr 22nd (overdubs),
May 16th (count-in intro)
Released on *Revolver*,
Aug 5th 1966 (UK),
Aug 8th 1966 (US)

Upon discovering that he was in the super-tax bracket, George Harrison decided that the only appropriate release for his anger was to write a song. Recorded within a week or two of the superb 'Rain', 'Taxman' is unsurprisingly Harrison's most aggressive composition, and McCartney answers the call to arms with another two-and-a-half minutes of brilliant, aggressive funk bass.

Where 'Rain' had quite a high level of improvisation and variation on the main groove, 'Taxman' is far more repetitive. 'Rain' lives at a slower tempo and, as such, was physically easier to play. McCartney felt more comfortable and more able to achieve a wider variety of ideas there. 'Taxman', however, is 20 beats-per-minute faster and so most of McCartney's effort goes into simply keeping the basic line solid, precise, and feeling good – no small achievement in this case.

The best place to hear the figure that McCartney employs for both verse and chorus is right at the front of the track (0:07). He hits the root on the first beat (in this case D) and the octave as two sixteenth-notes on the second. You can just hear the sixteenth-note pick-up (G) into the hammer-on that McCartney generally plays (other than in a few instances, and normally in the chorus, for example in bar 12, at 0:24). The hammer-on itself is always G to A, and it always ends up at the minor seventh (C in this case).

Although he always states the first beat of the bar in the verse and chorus with a solid quarter-note, there are variations in the middle of the bar. Have a listen to the funky counter-punch effect that McCartney gets from a solitary octave on the second beat of bars 39 (1:11) and 47 (1:25). Improvisation and variation can be about what you leave out as well as what you put in.

Most of the fourth beats (verse and chorus) are left empty. The space has the effect of efficiently demarcating the groove and, at the same time, injects an air of military precision into the proceedings. Obviously there are exceptions: heading into the chorus, he occasionally uses a cool, sliding quarter-note (for example bar 59, at 1:47). And check out the eighth-note pick-up that litters the final chorus (for example bar 74, at 2:16).

The verse is split into two four-bar sections and on the third bar of each McCartney plays the heavy accent along with the rest of the band, in place of the first half of his motif. He keeps it funky, however, by inserting the regular hammer-on lick in its usual place (for example bar 23, at 0:43).

In the bridge McCartney comes up with a groove that manages to retain the

overall theme but differentiate this section from the rest of the song. Check out bars 30 to 32 (0:55 to 1:00) and 34 to 36 (1:02 to 1:07): this is even more exciting than his main groove. It's only in the middle (bar 33 at 1:01) and right at the end of the bridge (bars 37 and 38 from 1:08 to 1:11), where Harrison's cynicism reaches a peak, that McCartney allows himself and the listener a bit of a breather.

The Beatles again use bluesy harmony in this song, so the home chord is D7, with a spiky sharp-ninth version emphasising the verse accents just discussed. This became known as the Hendrix chord because Jimi Hendrix would use it as the basis for songs like 'Purple Haze' and 'Voodoo Chile (Slight Return)'. As you can hear, it's laden with tension, and Harrison is using it to reflect the intensity of his anger. The C chords (for example bar 12 at 0:23) and F chords (bar 77 at 2:20), although not strictly from the key, are in keeping with the feel and generally bluesy vibe of the song. McCartney plays either his shifting verse/chorus shape or simple root notes until the bar before the fade-out guitar solo, when he slips in a neat scale run from F down to C, suggesting a key change that never actually happens.

Another major difference between 'Taxman' and 'Rain' is the minimal grace-note action here, although there's one notable exception at the end of the bridge (bar 37 into 38, from 1:09). McCartney identified the fact that a clean, clinical attack was appropriate to the subject matter, and overall this is an exercise in controlled repetition. He still delivers a few classy digressions such as the spiky fill into the second chorus (bar 24 at 0:45) and another into the fifth and final chorus (bar 72 at 2:11).

'Taxman' is a worthy culmination of a short period of recording where McCartney's technique seemed to take a massive leap. This is a hard-grooving, precise, finger-twister of a bassline and some world-class, kinetic funk playing that had very little precedent. Yet again McCartney set the template that many were to follow and yet again he recorded a superb bass part that still stands up today against anything else of its kind.

taxman

taxman

I'm Only Sleeping

verse 1 "When ..."

chorus 1 "Please ..."

verse 2 "Everybody ..."

chorus 2 "Please ..."

bridge 1 "Keeping ..."

verse 3 "Lying ..."

guitar solo

chorus 3 "Please ..."

bridge 2 "Keeping ..."

verse 4 "When ..."

chorus 4 "Please ..."

Recorded Apr 27th 1966, plus Apr 29th (lead vocal overdub), May 5th (backwards guitar overdubs), May 6th (overdubs)
Released on *Revolver*, Aug 5th 1966 (UK), Aug 8th 1966 (US)

This is another beautiful Lennon composition, from the dreamy haze somewhere between the conscious and unconscious states. Whether it's another one about drugs is neither clear nor conclusive, nor that important. What is important to us is that McCartney delivers another groove of masterful quality. We've chosen to transcribe and talk about this in the key of E, even though it sounds in E-flat (it was another victim of tape varispeeding, recorded in E and slowed down for effect).

The vibe is a sleazy shuffle, with McCartney pounding away on what sounds initially like simple quarter-notes, although closer inspection reveals more. McCartney's at it from bar 1, verse 1, in fact, where he states the E root note but immediately opens up the second half of the bar (0:02) with a stream of eighth-notes. He comes up with such a wealth of variation (for example bar 2 at 0:03, bar 5 at 0:11, and bar 7 at 0:16) that the bassline assumes an illusion of permanent improvisation, in much the same way as 'You Won't See Me', the variations in rhythmic approach giving the groove its slippery vibe. Check out the jazzy run-down that links verse and chorus using either a descending scalar pattern (for example bar 9 at 0:19) or a little contrary motion (bar 45 at 1:42 and bar 66 at 2:31).

The chorus sections see McCartney immediately adding a triplet to his repertoire (bar 10 at 0:22) without ever sounding like he's overdoing it, although the fourth chorus is something of a tour de force (bars 67 through 69, 2:34 to 2:41). A bass break climaxes each chorus but in three different lengths: for one bar (15 at 0:33, linking the first chorus and second verse); three bars (for example 30 through 32, 1:07 to 1:14, when a chorus is followed by a bridge); or two bars, just before the song finally dissolves in a haze of backwards guitar (72 through 73, 2:45 to 2:49).

Simple note choices (E minor arpeggio: E-G-B) married with a succulent feel and gloriously woody tone make this a little gem. An early 'songwriting' take on *Anthology 2* featuring Lennon and McCartney on acoustic guitars finds McCartney playing licks very close to the final bass phrase on acoustic, highlighting his ability to have a whole song (whether he wrote it or not) mapped out in advance of any serious attempts at recording.

There's a stricter plan in place for the two four-bar bridges. The first half of the first three bars simply has the root of each chord phrased in solid quarter-notes, while varied eighth and quarter-note ideas fill the second half. If you have a look at the transcription and make a visual comparison of bars 33 to 35 and bars 54 to 56 you'll see what we mean. Another solo bass lick adorns the fourth bar of each, but again it's more rhythmic spike than flashy lick, with the first (bar 36 at 1:21) slightly straighter in phrasing than the second (bar 57 at 2:10).

Aside from rhythmic embellishments, McCartney's attention to the detail of the note is in evidence with plenty of punchy, staccato phrasing (for example bar 10 at 0:21 and bar 55 at 2:05). This helps reinforce both the acoustic element of his tone, by simulating the more rapid note decay of an upright bass, and the forward motion of the groove. There are a few grace notes (for example bar 68 at 2:36) and slides (for example bar 25 into 26 at 0:58) but these are ornamentations and not essential to the bassline.

McCartney's groove here is about feel, rhythm, and tone. He's after a laidback feel that will complement Lennon's concept and, with the help of Starr, this is what he achieves, effortlessly. The swing rhythm gives him the opportunity to try out a slightly jazzier approach both rhythmically and tonally, and it's a testament to his level of confidence and belief that he pulls it off – even if the bass sound we're left with is somewhat indistinct and buried in places.

i'm only sleeping

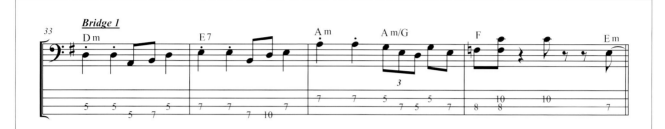

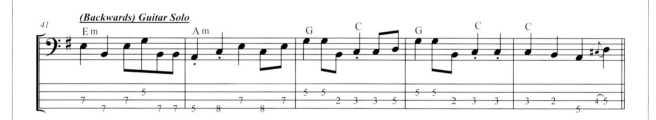

i'm only sleeping

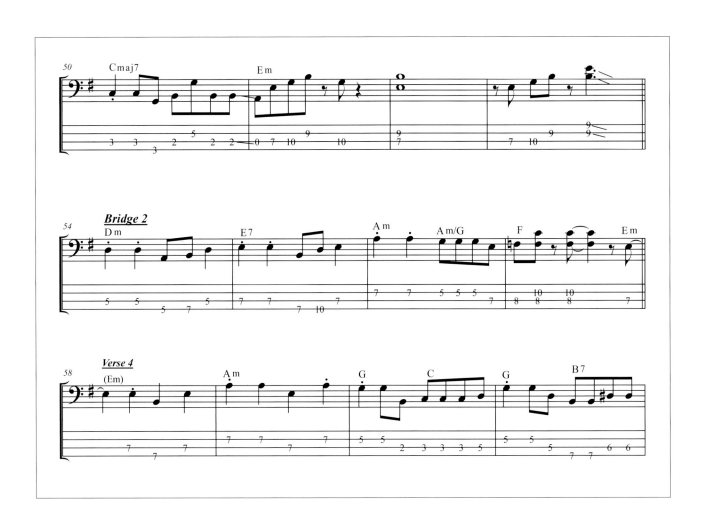

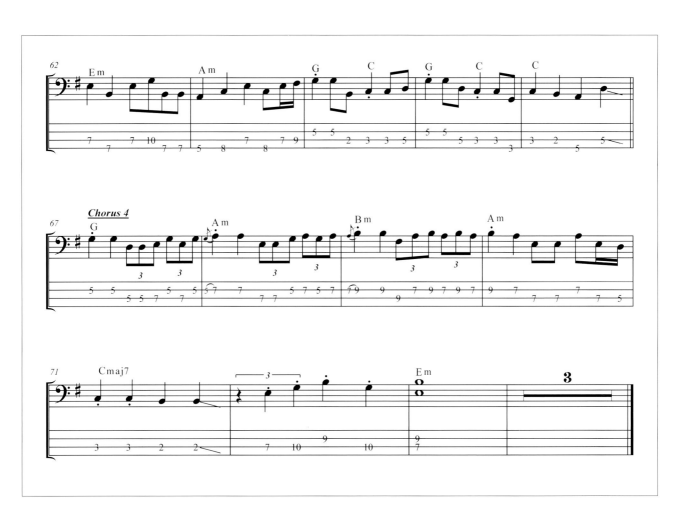

Lovely Rita

chorus 1 "Lovely Rita meter ..." x2
verse 1 "Lovely Rita ... nothing ..."
chorus 2 "Lovely Rita... take ..."
piano solo
verse 2 "Took her out..."
chorus 3 "Lovely Rita... where ..."
outro

Recorded Feb 23rd 1967,
plus Feb 24th (lead vocal
overdub), Mar 7th
(overdubs), Mar 21st
(piano solo overdub)
Released on *Sgt Pepper's
Lonely Hearts Club Band*,
Jun 1st 1967 (UK),
Jun 2nd 1967 (US)

This is one of McCartney's more playful compositions, concerning the attempts of a young man to get out of paying a ticket by wining and dining the parking attendant. It's another recording where the tape speed was slowed, with the released version residing just sharp of E flat, though it was recorded in the key of E, which is where we're placing it for this transcription and discussion.

'Rita' definitely benefits from McCartney's new-found luxury of adding bass after the recording had taken a firm shape, especially as he's able to gauge the most effective way of approaching the unusual verse structure: two three-bar sequences and a tag bar. The choice of notes is nothing new, based on a 'walking bass' mix of scale and arpeggio, but the Rickenbacker gives him more clarity and a richer tone that help inject the funk into what would otherwise be a fairly workmanlike groove.

Although there's plenty of repetition, if you compare the first bar of each verse it will give you an idea of the subtle and classy variations McCartney employs. In the first verse (bar 13 at 0:33) all eight notes are staccato; in the second, although the melodic choices are very similar, McCartney throws in a sixteenth-note lick and keeps the notes long in the first half of the bar (bar 31 at 1:22), noticeably altering the feel. He keeps it simple for both tag bars, which are jazz/blues-derived 'turnarounds', using root notes the first time (bar 19 at 0:49) and adding a virtually inaudible variation (bar 37 at 1:39) the second, almost as if he's striving to minimise strict repetition other than in certain designated places.

One of those places occurs after the opening four bars of piano. McCartney's groove under the "lovely Rita, meter maid" refrain feels more static than what follows but also more sophisticated and ultra cool. He does this by injecting some contrary motion into the arpeggios, resulting in a root-third-root-fifth sequence (bar 5 from 0:11), and letting the fourth note drift away from its initial pitch (bar 6 at 0:17), which lends a sleazy yet sophisticated edge to proceedings. He makes good use of this phrase, revisiting it in slightly altered form in the chorus, either with different notes but a pretty straight phrasing 'lift' (bar 20 at 0:52) or mixed with quarter-notes (bar 38 at 1:41). Have a listen to the outro version where he plays exactly the same notes as the intro but slightly juggles the phrasing, gracing to the root and stunting the length of the second note (for example bar 45 at 2:01).

Close to the end, McCartney plays a funky, single-bar figure eight times (from

2:11 to 2:33). As there's very little precise repetition of bass ideas in 'Rita' we expect some degree of improvisation – but it never comes. The choice of chord and the quirky left-field nature of the accompanying bass part is very much like one of those detective novels where a character appears without preamble in the last quarter of the tale and proves to be responsible for everything that has preceded their entrance. The phrase has no precedent, and neither does the chord. Perhaps it's there simply to keep us guessing? Or maybe the darker mood of this little snippet has an importance in terms of the lyrical narrative? McCartney has again provided us with something that's fun to listen to but also makes us think.

The chorus stays pretty close to the home key of E defined in the song's opening vamp. In the verses, the chords move towards a modulation, though this is never really established, and in this instance McCartney takes the opportunity to highlight the slight alteration to both key and scale, notably by playing a C underneath the D chord riff when C-sharp would be more 'correct' (for example bar 14 at 0:35, bar 32 at 1:25, and bar 35 at 1:33). It helps maintain the bluesy funk vibe – C-sharp would have sounded too sweet – and shows how much thought McCartney put into even the simplest of ideas at this stage in his career.

'Rita' is an excellent piece of driving groove-playing by McCartney and another song from this period where the bass is the leading melodic contributor after the vocal. In the context of the majority of pop music of this time, it was nothing short of revolutionary. The variations of phrasing and approach contained within the 2 minutes 40 seconds combined with the progressive chord structure and rabbit-out-of-a-hat section at the end showed that the creative possibilities of the humble pop song and the opportunities for the bassist to play expressively were nowhere near exhausted. In fact, the horizon was expanding rapidly thanks mainly to one Liverpudlian bass maestro.

Dear Prudence

verse 1 "Dear Prudence, won't ..."

verse 2 "Dear Prudence, open ..."

bridge "Look ..."

verse 3 "Dear Prudence, let ..."

verse 4 (outro) "Dear Prudence, won't ..."

Recorded Aug 28th 1968,
plus Aug 29th (overdubs,
inc bass)
Released on *The Beatles*,
Nov 22nd 1968 (UK),
Nov 25th 1968 (US)

Lennon wrote this moody classic about how Mia Farrow's sister was unwilling to leave her hut in Rishikesh during The Beatles' Indian studies with the Maharishi. McCartney delivers a bassline that manages to capture the mood perfectly and stands out as one of his finest stylistic statements.

There's plenty of melody in the guitar arpeggiation and McCartney allows this to bed-in for more than 40 seconds, restricting his accompaniment to a chiming octave (for example bar 7 at 0:20) that matches the serenity of Lennon's vocal and maximises the impact when he finally starts the main groove halfway through the first verse, at 0:44. Even then, this first version is less weighty than what he will play later in the song.

The static chord with the descending bassline motif gives both a foundation for the groove and provides an obvious melodic shape from which McCartney fashions his highly unusual masterwork. Starting on the fifth (A), he then states the root before sliding up to the octave, drops down to the next bass note in time with the guitar, and heads back to the root (for example bar 8 at 0:44). He then repeats this process over the remainder of the two-bar sequence, using the respective octave of each bass note as his falling-away point. It's a lot simpler than this reads, and injects a brooding intention underneath Lennon's floating vocal.

The second and third verses are more full-blooded affairs with McCartney pumping away on eighth-notes (for example bar 14 at 1:03). The real genius here is that this busier approach gives the phrases much less time to speak – but we don't really notice.

McCartney ditches the riff in favour of melodic scale fragments at the end of the first verse over the climactic chord changes (bar 11 at 0:53), but in the second and third verses he chooses to break the main groove down before the changes. For verse two he strips down his main idea to root notes only, and his injection of space into the descending hook shows a real mastery of the oft-ignored art of dynamics (bar 22 through 23 from 1:29 to 1:35). In the third verse he keeps the eighth-notes pumping, adding a little colour through the descending sequence (bars 41 through 42 from 2:37 to 2:43) as the guitar overdubs start to appear. This effectively leads the listener to the culminating verse (four) where McCartney reclaims the broken motif he used earlier (for example bar 47 through 48 from 2:55 to 3:01). He has the common sense to radically diminish the melodic content of the bass part, allowing the increasing number of overdubbed guitar phrases to dominate. The last five bars of groove have a funky walking-bass quality with a cool chromatic lick at 3:21 and some effective scalar phrases (for example bar 57 at 3:24).

Although the bridge-section groove is closely related to the sinewy verse offering, it simply doubles the rhythm guitar part (for example bar 28 at 1:48). It's a bit of a chicken-and-egg question, but could McCartney's bassline have been the basis for what Lennon played on rhythm guitar, thus representing a major creative contribution? We'll never know for sure, but what is certain is that he makes the idea his own through sheer strength of phrasing, especially by squeezing out every fourth note (octave D) with a C-sharp grace note.

'Prudence' is in the key of D, with the descending bassline drawn directly from the turnaround in a 12-bar blues. In other words, in the second-last bar of a blues in D, one option is to play a descending bassline, and the choice of notes would always be D, C, B, and B-flat (resolving to A) under a pedal D chord – which is exactly what Lennon is doing here. The fact that it never resolves creates a lot of tension. In the fifth bar of the bridge (bar 29 at 2:01) Lennon throws a brief minor-third cycle into the pot (F followed by A-flat) but McCartney chooses to underpin this (and the superb stacked backing vocal) with simple eighth-notes, although there is one neat chromatic lick in bar 30 (2:04).

'Dear Prudence' is a masterful piece of rock-funk. It's all about the way McCartney turns a simple groove into one of the most sophisticated sounding parts he ever recorded with The Beatles. Yet again he determines the character of a superb Lennon composition and yet again his contribution is the most important element after Lennon's vocal.

dear prudence

reference

discography

This discography is in two parts. The first section ('Song By Song') details the EMI studio tracks officially released on CD along with recording dates and bass data; the second section ('Original Records') organises the contemporary singles, EPs and LPs in order of their release date.

Song By Song

Here we list all of The Beatles' studio recordings officially released on CD. The database is designed to help you find a particular song on a particular disc, along with some extra information. It's organised by song title in alphabetical order. A few multiple versions are shown where relevant. Following the title are the CD on which the track first appeared, the recording date(s), the bassist on the track (mostly McCartney, 'PM', of course, but there are exceptions), and the bass guitar we think was most likely to have been used. ('H1' means McCartney's first 'close-pickups' Hofner 500/1; 'H2' is his second Hofner 500/1, the 'conventional pickups' instrument; and 'R' indicates his Rickenbacker 4001S. 'F6' is the Fender VI six-string bass, mostly played by Lennon, 'JL', or Harrison, 'GH'.)

A DAY IN THE LIFE
Sgt Pepper | Jan/Feb/Mar 67 | PM | R

A HARD DAY'S NIGHT
Hard Day's Night | Apr 64 | PM | H2

A TASTE OF HONEY
Please Please Me | Feb 63 | PM | H1

ACROSS THE UNIVERSE (no strings etc)
Let It Be Naked | Feb 68 | no bass | –

ACROSS THE UNIVERSE (strings etc)
Past Masters 2 | Feb 68/Apr 70 | no bass | –

ACT NATURALLY
Help! | Jun 65 | PM | H2

AIN'T SHE SWEET
Anthology 1 | Jun 61 | PM | H1

ALL I'VE GOT TO DO
With The Beatles | Sep 63 | PM | H1

ALL MY LOVING
With The Beatles | Jul 63 | PM | H1

ALL TOGETHER NOW
Yellow Submarine | May 67 | PM | R

ALL YOU NEED IS LOVE
Magical Mystery Tour | Jun 67 | PM | R

AND I LOVE HER
Hard Day's Night | Feb 64 | PM | H2

AND YOUR BIRD CAN SING
Revolver | Apr 66 | PM | R

ANNA (GO TO HIM)
Please Please Me | Feb 63 | PM | H1

ANOTHER GIRL
Help! | Feb 65 | PM | H2

ANY TIME AT ALL
Hard Day's Night | Jun 64 | PM | H2

ASK ME WHY
Please Please Me | Jun/Nov 62 | PM | H1

BABY IT'S YOU
Please Please Me | Feb 63 | PM | H1

BABY YOU'RE A RICH MAN
Magical Mystery Tour | May 67 | PM | R

BABY'S IN BLACK
Beatles For Sale | Aug 64 | PM | H2

BACK IN THE USSR
White Album | Aug 68 | JL | F6

BAD BOY
Past Masters 1 | May 65 | PM | H2

BALLAD OF JOHN AND YOKO
see THE BALLAD OF JOHN AND YOKO

BECAUSE
Abbey Road | Aug 69 | PM | R

BEING FOR THE BENEFIT OF MR KITE
Sgt Pepper | Feb/Mar 67 | PM | R

BESAME MUCHO
Anthology 1 | Jun 62 | PM | H1

BIRTHDAY
White Album | Sep 68 | GH (JL?) | F6

BLACKBIRD
White Album | Jun 68 | no bass | –

BLUE JAY WAY
Magical Mystery Tour | Sep/Oct 67 | PM | R

BOYS
Please Please Me | Feb 63 | PM | H1

CAN'T BUY ME LOVE
Hard Day's Night | Jan/Feb/Mar 64 | PM | H2

CARRY THAT WEIGHT
Abbey Road | Jul/Aug 69 | PM | R

CHAINS
Please Please Me | Feb 63 | PM | H1

COME TOGETHER
Abbey Road | Jul 69 | PM | R

CONTINUING STORY OF BUNGALOW BILL
see THE CONTINUING STORY OF BUNGALOW BILL

CRY BABY CRY
White Album | Jul 68 | PM | R

CRY FOR A SHADOW				
Anthology 1	Jun 61	PM		H1
DAY TRIPPER				
Past Masters 2	Oct 65	PM		H2
DAY IN THE LIFE				
see A DAY IN THE LIFE				
DEAR PRUDENCE				
White Album	Aug 68	PM		R
DEVIL IN HER HEART				
With The Beatles	Jul 63	PM		H1
DIG A PONY				
Let It Be	Jan 69	PM		H2
DIG IT				
Let It Be	Jan 69	PM		H2
DIZZY MISS LIZZY				
Help!	May 65	PM		H2
DO YOU WANT TO KNOW A SECRET				
Please Please Me	Feb 63	PM		H1
DOCTOR ROBERT				
Revolver	Apr 66	PM		R
DON'T BOTHER ME				
With The Beatles	Sep 63	PM		H1
DON'T LET ME DOWN				
Past Masters 2	Jan 69	PM		H2
DON'T PASS ME BY				
White Album	Jun/Jul 68	PM		R
DRIVE MY CAR				
Rubber Soul	Oct 65	PM		R
EIGHT DAYS A WEEK				
Beatles For Sale	Oct 64	PM		H2
ELEANOR RIGBY				
Revolver	Apr/Jun 66	no bass		–
EVERY LITTLE THING				
Beatles For Sale	Sep 64	PM		H2
EVERYBODY'S GOT SOMETHING TO HIDE EXCEPT ME AND MY MONKEY				
White Album	Jun/Jul 68	PM		R
EVERYBODY'S TRYING TO BE MY BABY				
Beatles For Sale	Oct 64	PM		H2
FIXING A HOLE				
Sgt Pepper	Feb 67	PM		R
FLYING				
Magical Mystery Tour	Sep 67	PM		R
FOOL ON THE HILL				
see THE FOOL ON THE HILL				
FOR NO ONE				
Revolver	May 66	PM		R
FOR YOU BLUE				
Let It Be	Jan 69/Jan 70	no bass		–
FROM ME TO YOU				
Past Masters 1	Mar 63	PM		H1
GET BACK (album take)				
Let It Be	Jan 69	PM		H2
GET BACK (single take)				
Past Masters 2	Jan 69	PM		H2
GETTING BETTER				
Sgt Pepper	Mar 67	PM		R
GIRL				
Rubber Soul	Nov 65	PM		R
GLASS ONION				
White Album	Sep/Oct 68	JL (GH?)		F6
GOLDEN SLUMBERS				
Abbey Road	Jul/Aug 69	PM		R
GOOD DAY SUNSHINE				
Revolver	Jun 66	PM		R
GOOD MORNING GOOD MORNING				
Sgt Pepper	Feb/Mar 67	PM		R
GOOD NIGHT				
White Album	Jun/Jul 68	no bass		–
GOT TO GET YOU INTO MY LIFE				
Revolver	Apr/May/Jun 66	PM		R
HAPPINESS IS A WARM GUN				
White Album	Sep 68	PM		R
HARD DAY'S NIGHT				
see A HARD DAY'S NIGHT				
HELLO GOODBYE				
Magical Mystery Tour	Oct/Nov 67	PM		R
HELLO LITTLE GIRL				
Anthology 1	Jan 62	PM		H1
HELP!				
Help!	Apr 65	PM		H2
HELTER SKELTER				
White Album	Jul/Sep 68	JL (PM?)		F6
HER MAJESTY				
Abbey Road	Jul 69	no bass		–
HERE COMES THE SUN				
Abbey Road	Jul/Aug 69	PM		R
HERE THERE AND EVERYWHERE				
Revolver	Jun 66	PM		R
HEY BULLDOG				
Yellow Submarine	Feb 68	PM		R
HEY JUDE				
Past Masters 2	Jul/Aug 68	PM		R
HOLD ME TIGHT				
With The Beatles	Feb/Sep 63	PM		H1
HONEY DON'T				
Beatles For Sale	Oct 64	PM		H2
HONEY PIE				
White Album	Oct 68	GH (JL?)		F6
HOW DO YOU DO IT				
Anthology 1	Sep 62	PM		H1
I AM THE WALRUS				
Magical Mystery Tour	Sep 67	PM		R
I CALL YOUR NAME				
Past Masters 1	Mar 64	PM		H2
I DON'T WANT TO SPOIL THE PARTY				
Beatles For Sale	Sep 64	PM		H2
I FEEL FINE				
Past Masters 1	Oct 64	PM		H2
I ME MINE				
Let It Be	Jan/Apr 70	PM		H2
I NEED YOU				
Help!	Feb 65	PM		H2
I SAW HER STANDING THERE				
Please Please Me	Feb 63	PM		H1
I SHOULD HAVE KNOWN BETTER				
Hard Day's Night	Feb 64	PM		H2
I WANNA BE YOUR MAN				
With The Beatles	Sep/Oct 63	PM		H1
I WANT TO HOLD YOUR HAND				
Past Masters 1	Oct 63	PM		H2
I WANT TO TELL YOU				
Revolver	Jun 66	PM		R
I WANT YOU (SHE'S SO HEAVY)				
Abbey Road	Feb/Apr/Aug 69	PM		H2
I WILL				
White Album	Sep 68	no bass		–
IF I FELL				
Hard Day's Night	Feb 64	PM		H2
IF I NEEDED SOMEONE				
Rubber Soul	Oct 65	PM		R
IF YOU'VE GOT TROUBLE				
Anthology 2	Feb 65	PM		H2
I'LL BE BACK				
Hard Day's Night	Jun 64	PM		H2
I'LL CRY INSTEAD				
Hard Day's Night	Jun 64	PM		H2
I'LL FOLLOW THE SUN				
Beatles For Sale	Oct 64	PM		H2
I'LL GET YOU				
Past Masters 1	Jul 63	PM		H1
I'M A LOSER				
Beatles For Sale	Aug 64	PM		H2

Song	Album	Date	Writer	Code
I'M DOWN	Past Masters 1	Jun 65	PM	H2
I'M HAPPY JUST TO DANCE WITH YOU	Hard Day's Night	Mar 64	PM	H2
I'M LOOKING THROUGH YOU	Rubber Soul Oct/Nov 65		PM	R
I'M ONLY SLEEPING	Revolver	Apr/May 66	PM	R
I'M SO TIRED	White Album	Oct 68	PM	R
IN MY LIFE	Rubber Soul	Oct 65	PM	R
INNER LIGHT see THE INNER LIGHT				
IT WON'T BE LONG	With The Beatles	Jul 63	PM	H1
IT'S ALL TOO MUCH	Yellow Submarine	May/Jun 67	PM	R
IT'S ONLY LOVE	Help!	Jun 65	PM	H2
I'VE GOT A FEELING	Let It Be	Jan 69	PM	H2
I'VE JUST SEEN A FACE	Help!	Jun 65	PM	H2
JULIA	White Album	Oct 68	no bass	–
KANSAS CITY/HEY, HEY, HEY, HEY	Beatles For Sale	Oct 64	PM	H2
LADY MADONNA	Past Masters 2	Feb 68	PM	R
LEAVE MY KITTEN ALONE	Anthology 1	Aug 64	PM	H2
LET IT BE (Jan 69 gtr solo)	Let It Be Naked	Jan 69	JL	F6
LET IT BE (Apr gtr solo)	Past Masters 2	Jan/Apr 69	JL	F6
LET IT BE (Jan 70 gtr solo)	Let It Be	Jan 69/Jan 70	JL	F6
LIKE DREAMERS DO	Anthology 1	Jan 62	PM	H1
LITTLE CHILD	With The Beatles	Sep/Oct 63	PM	H1
LONG AND WINDING ROAD see THE LONG AND WINDING ROAD				
LONG LONG LONG	White Album	Oct 68	PM	R
LONG TALL SALLY	Past Masters 1	Mar 64	PM	H2
LOVE ME DO (Best dr)	Anthology 1	Jun 62	PM	H1
LOVE ME DO (Starr dr)	Past Masters 1	Sep 62	PM	H1
LOVE ME DO (White dr)	Please Please Me	Sep 62	PM	H1
LOVE YOU TO	Revolver	Apr 66	no bass	–
LOVELY RITA	Sgt Pepper	Feb/Mar 67	PM	R
LUCY IN THE SKY WITH DIAMONDS	Sgt Pepper	Feb/Mar 67	PM	R
MAGGIE MAE	Let It Be	Jan 69	no bass	–
MAGICAL MYSTERY TOUR	Magical Mystery Tour	Apr/May/Nov 67	PM	R
MARTHA MY DEAR	White Album	Oct 68	PM	R
MATCHBOX	Past Masters 1	Jun 64	PM	H2
MAXWELL'S SILVER HAMMER	Abbey Road	Jul/Aug 69	PM	R
MEAN MR MUSTARD	Abbey Road	Jul 69	PM	R
MICHELLE	Rubber Soul	Nov 65	PM	R
MISERY	Please Please Me	Feb 63	PM	H1
MONEY	With The Beatles	Jul/Sep 63	PM	H1
MOTHER NATURE'S SON	White Album	Aug 68	no bass	–
MR. MOONLIGHT	Beatles For Sale	Aug/Oct 64	PM	H2
MY BONNIE	Anthology 1	Jun 61	PM	H1
NO REPLY	Beatles For Sale	Jun/Sep 64	PM	H2
NORWEGIAN WOOD (THIS BIRD HAS FLOWN)	Rubber Soul	Oct 65	PM	R
NOT A SECOND TIME	With The Beatles	Sep 63	PM	H1
NOT GUILTY	Anthology 3	Aug 68	PM	R
NOWHERE MAN	Rubber Soul	Oct 65	PM	R
OB-LA-DI OB-LA-DA	White Album	Jul 68	PM	R
OCTOPUS'S GARDEN	Abbey Road	Apr/Jul 69	PM	H2
OH! DARLING	Abbey Road	Jan/Apr/Jul/Aug 69	PM	H2
OLD BROWN SHOE	Past Masters 2	Feb/Apr 69	PM	H2
ONE AFTER 909 (early)	Anthology 1	Mar 63	PM	H1
ONE AFTER 909 (later)	Let It Be	Jan 69	PM	H2
ONLY A NORTHERN SONG	Yellow Submarine	Feb/Apr 67	PM	R
PAPERBACK WRITER	Past Masters 2	Apr 66	PM	R
PENNY LANE	Magical Mystery Tour	Dec 66/Jan 67	PM	R
PIGGIES	White Album	Sep/Oct 68	PM	R
PLEASE MISTER POSTMAN	With The Beatles	Jul 63	PM	H1
PLEASE PLEASE ME (White dr)	Anthology 1	Sep 62	PM	H1
PLEASE PLEASE ME (Starr dr)	Please Please Me	Nov 62	PM	H1
POLYTHENE PAM	Abbey Road	Jul 69	PM	R
P.S. I LOVE YOU	Please Please Me	Jun/Sep 62	PM	H1
RAIN	Past Masters 2	Apr 66	PM	R
REVOLUTION	Past Masters 2	Jul 68	PM	R
REVOLUTION 1	White Album	May/Jun 68	PM	R
REVOLUTION 9	White Album	Jun 68	no bass	–
ROCK AND ROLL MUSIC	Beatles For Sale	Oct 64	PM	H2
ROCKY RACCOON	White Album	Aug 68	JL	F6
ROLL OVER BEETHOVEN	With The Beatles	Jul 63	PM	H1
RUN FOR YOUR LIFE	Rubber Soul	Oct 65	PM	R
SAVOY TRUFFLE	White Album	Oct 68	PM	R
SEARCHIN'	Anthology 1	Jan 62	PM	H1

Song	Album	Date	Bass	Ref
SEXY SADIE	White Album	Jul/Aug 68	PM	R
SGT PEPPER'S LONELY HEARTS CLUB BAND	Sgt Pepper	Feb/Mar 67	PM	R
SGT PEPPER'S LONELY HEARTS CLUB BAND (REPRISE)	Sgt Pepper	Apr 67	PM	R
SHE CAME IN THROUGH THE BATHROOM WINDOW	Abbey Road	Jul 69	PM	R
SHE LOVES YOU	Past Masters 1	Jul 63	PM	H1
SHE SAID SHE SAID	Revolver	Jun 66	PM	R
SHEIK OF ARABY see THE SHEIK OF ARABY				
SHE'S A WOMAN	Past Masters 1	Oct 64	PM	H2
SHE'S LEAVING HOME	Sgt Pepper	Mar 67	no bass	–
SLOW DOWN	Past Masters 1	Jun 64	PM	H2
SOMETHING	Abbey Road	Feb/Apr/May/Jul/Aug 69	PM	R
STRAWBERRY FIELDS FOREVER	Magical Mystery Tour	Nov/Dec 66	PM	R
SUN KING	Abbey Road	Jul 69	PM	R
TASTE OF HONEY see A TASTE OF HONEY				
TAXMAN	Revolver	Apr/May 66	PM	R
TELL ME WHAT YOU SEE	Help!	Feb 65	PM	H2
TELL ME WHY	Hard Day's Night	Feb 64	PM	H2
THANK YOU GIRL	Past Masters 1	Mar 63	PM	H1
THAT MEANS A LOT	Anthology 2	Feb 65	PM	H2
THE BALLAD OF JOHN AND YOKO	Past Masters 2	Apr 69	PM	H2
THE CONTINUING STORY OF BUNGALOW BILL	White Album	Oct 68	PM	R
THE END	Abbey Road	Jul/Aug 69	PM	R
THE FOOL ON THE HILL	Magical Mystery Tour	Sep/Oct 67	PM	R
THE INNER LIGHT	Past Masters 2	Jan/Feb 68	no bass	–
THE LONG AND WINDING ROAD (Jan 26, no strings etc)	Anthology 3	Jan 69	JL	F6
THE LONG AND WINDING ROAD (Jan 31, no strings etc)	Let It Be Naked	Jan 69	JL	F6
THE LONG AND WINDING ROAD (Jan 26 + strings etc)	Let It Be	Jan 69/Apr 70	JL	F6
THE NIGHT BEFORE	Help!	Feb 65	PM	H2
THE SHEIK OF ARABY	Anthology 1	Jan 62	PM	H1
THE WORD	Rubber Soul	Nov 65	PM	R
THERE'S A PLACE	Please Please Me	Feb 63	PM	H1
THINGS WE SAID TODAY	Hard Day's Night	Jun 64	PM	H2
THINK FOR YOURSELF	Rubber Soul	Nov 65	PM	R
THIS BOY	Past Masters 1	Oct 63	PM	H2
THREE COOL CATS	Anthology 1	Jan 62	PM	H1
TICKET TO RIDE	Help!	Feb 65	PM	H2
TILL THERE WAS YOU	With The Beatles	Jul 63	PM	H1
TOMORROW NEVER KNOWS	Revolver	Apr 66	PM	R
12-BAR ORIGINAL	Anthology 2	Nov 65	PM	R
TWIST AND SHOUT	Please Please Me	Feb 63	PM	H1
TWO OF US	Let It Be	Jan 69	GH	F6
WAIT	Rubber Soul	Jun/Nov 65	PM	H2
WE CAN WORK IT OUT	Past Masters 2	Oct 65	PM	R
WHAT GOES ON	Rubber Soul	Nov 65	PM	R
WHAT YOU'RE DOING	Beatles For Sale	Sep/Oct 64	PM	H2
WHAT'S THE NEW MARY JANE	Anthology 3	Aug 68	no bass	–
WHEN I GET HOME	Hard Day's Night	Jun 64	PM	H2
WHEN I'M SIXTY-FOUR	Sgt Pepper	Dec 66	PM	R
WHILE MY GUITAR GENTLY WEEPS	White Album	Aug/Sep 68	PM	R
WHY DON'T WE DO IT IN THE ROAD	White Album	Oct 68	PM	R
WILD HONEY PIE	White Album	Aug 68	no bass	–
WITH A LITTLE HELP FROM MY FRIENDS	Sgt Pepper	Mar 67	PM	R
WITHIN YOU WITHOUT YOU	Sgt Pepper	Mar/Apr 67	no bass	–
WORDS OF LOVE	Beatles For Sale	Oct 64	PM	H2
YELLOW SUBMARINE	Revolver	May/Jun 66	PM	R
YER BLUES	White Album	Aug 68	PM	R
YES IT IS	Past Masters 1	Feb 65	PM	H2
YESTERDAY	Help!	Jun 65	no bass	–
YOU CAN'T DO THAT	Hard Day's Night	Feb/May 64	PM	H2
YOU KNOW MY NAME (LOOK UP THE NUMBER)	Past Masters 2	May/Jun 67/Apr 69	PM	R
YOU LIKE ME TOO MUCH	Help!	Feb 65	PM	H2
YOU NEVER GIVE ME YOUR MONEY	Abbey Road	May/Jul/Aug 69	PM	R
YOU REALLY GOT A HOLD ON ME	With The Beatles	Jul/Oct 63	PM	H1
YOU WON'T SEE ME	Rubber Soul	Nov 65	PM	R
YOUR MOTHER SHOULD KNOW	Magical Mystery Tour	Aug/Sep 67	PM	R
YOU'RE GOING TO LOSE THAT GIRL	Help!	Feb/Mar 65	PM	H2
YOU'VE GOT TO HIDE YOUR LOVE AWAY	Help!	Feb 65	PM	H2

original records

Contemporary official releases of EMI recordings are listed here to show the record title – single A-side ('In Single Quotes'), EP (No Quotes), or album (*In Italics*) – followed by release month. A single month alone indicates a record released in the same month in the UK and the US; two different months separated by a slash indicates a record released at different times in the UK/US; and a single month followed by 'UK' or 'US' means the record was only released in that country.

1962
'Love Me Do' Oct UK

1963
'Please Please Me' Jan/Feb
Please Please Me Mar UK
'From Me To You' Apr/May
Twist and Shout Jul UK
'She Loves You' Aug/Sep
The Beatles Hits Sep UK
'I Want To Hold Your Hand' Nov/Dec
The Beatles (No.1) Nov UK
With The Beatles Nov UK

1964
Introducing The Beatles Jan US
Meet The Beatles! Jan US
All My Loving Feb UK
'Twist And Shout' Feb US
'Can't Buy Me Love' Mar
'Do You Want To Know A Secret' Mar US
Souvenir Of Their Visit To America Mar US

'Love Me Do' Apr US
The Beatles' Second Album Apr US
Four By The Beatles May US
Long Tall Sally Jun UK
A Hard Day's Night (US version) Jun US
'A Hard Day's Night' Jul
A Hard Day's Night (UK version) Jul UK
'I'll Cry Instead' Jul US
'And I Love Her' Jul US
Something New Jul US
'Matchbox' Aug US
'I Feel Fine' Nov
Extracts From The Album A Hard Day's Night Nov UK
Extracts From The Film A Hard Day's Night Nov UK
Beatles For Sale Dec UK
Beatles '65 Dec US

1965
'Eight Days A Week' Feb US
4 By The Beatles Feb US
The Early Beatles Mar US
'Ticket To Ride' Apr
Beatles For Sale Apr UK
Beatles For Sale No.2 Jun UK
Beatles VI Jun US
'Help!' Jul
Help! (UK version) Aug UK
Help! (US version) Aug US
'Yesterday' Sep US
'We Can Work It Out'/'Day Tripper' Dec
The Beatles' Million Sellers Dec UK
Rubber Soul (UK version) Dec UK
Rubber Soul (US version) Dec US

1966
'Nowhere Man' Feb US
Yesterday Mar UK
'Paperback Writer' Jun/May
"Yesterday" ... And Today Jun US
Nowhere Man Jul UK
'Yellow Submarine'/'Eleanor Rigby' Aug
Revolver (UK version) Aug UK
Revolver (US version) Aug US
A Collection Of Beatles Oldies Dec UK

1967
'Strawberry Fields Forever'/'Penny Lane' Feb
Sgt Pepper's Lonely Hearts Club Band Jun
'All You Need Is Love' Jul
'Hello Goodbye' Nov
Magical Mystery Tour Nov US
Magical Mystery Tour Dec UK

1968
'Lady Madonna' Mar
'Hey Jude' Aug
The Beatles ('*The White Album*') Nov

1969
Yellow Submarine Jan
'Get Back' Apr/May
'The Ballad Of John And Yoko' May/Jun
Abbey Road Sep/Oct
'Something'/'Come Together' Oct

1970
Hey Jude Feb US
'Let It Be' Mar
'The Long And Winding Road' May US
Let It Be May

Later collections referred to in the Song By Song listing and in the main text include *Past Masters Volume One* and *Past Masters Volume Two* (Mar 1988), which rounded up songs not available elsewhere on CD at the time, the three out-takes and oddities sets *Anthology 1* (Nov 1995), *Anthology 2* (Mar 1996), and *Anthology 3* (Oct 1996), and the revised and de-Spector'd *Let It Be ... Naked* (Nov 2003). In the general text of the book, we refer to the *Live At The BBC* two-CD set (Nov/Dec 1994) and to some recordings on a couple of concert vinyl-only albums: *Live! At The Star-Club In Hamburg Germany; 1962* (May 1977 UK; May/Jun 1977 US) and *The Beatles At The Hollywood Bowl* (May 1977).

glossary

ACCENT. Indicated with this symbol above the note in standard notation (not tab). It means you should play the note a little louder than normal.

ALTERED CHORD. A chord that includes a note or notes not from the parent scale or key.

ARPEGGIO. Playing the notes of a chord individually, usually in order from lowest to highest pitch.

BLUES SCALE. A variation on the minor pentatonic (root, minor third, fourth, fifth, minor seventh; for example, the G blues scale consists of G, Bb, C, D, F) with the sharpened fourth added (C# in the example).

CHROMATIC NOTE. One that does not belong to the parent scale or key.

DOUBLE-STOP. Playing two notes at the same time, for colour or effect.

GLISSANDO. See slide.

GRACE NOTE. In notation this is printed as a 'miniature' note, and in tab as a miniature number. It's a note that 'graces' or ornaments the main notes of a melody, purely for decoration. A grace note doesn't alter the rhythm, however; it takes time from the note it joins on to, so the pulse remains the same.

HAMMER-ON. In notation, two notes of different pitches connected by a bowed line. Play the first conventionally, then sound the second with a fretting-hand finger only.

LEGATO. When written, an instruction to play a phrase smoothly, with notes given their full written values. In standard notation, where a phrase contains both legato and staccato notes, notes to be played at their full value have a short line over them, technically a tenuto mark. It is also known as a legato mark.

MODULATION. Moving from one key to another.

OCTAVE. The distance between the first and eighth notes of a scale: both have the same letter name; the second is double the frequency of the first.

PEDAL. The effect when a bass note is deliberately repeated (or sustained) against changing harmony.

PICK-UP. Not the thing bolted to the bass, but a note or figure just before a downbeat or repeated phrase, leading to it.

RALLENTANDO or **RAL.** Indicated on standard notation (not tab) as shown in the example. It means to gradually slow down, from the start of the bracketed section.

RIFF. A melodic phrase or chord sequence that is repeated regularly throughout a song.

ROOT. The note upon which a chord is based, and which provides its letter name.

SCALE. Group of seven notes arranged in alphabetical order with a set pattern of intervals (the distances between notes). The term is also applied generically to various sequences of notes (see, for example, 'blues scale' here).

SLIDE or **GLISSANDO.** Shown in notation and tab as a straight line connecting the two relevant notes and meaning that you should slide smoothly up or down from one note to the next.

STACCATO. In standard notation (not tab) this is shown as a dot underneath or above the note (depending on which way the stem is going) and means to clip the note to about half its written value.

TAG BAR. An extra bar or bars inserted between sections.

TENUTO. See legato.

TRIAD. A simple chord consisting of root, third, and fifth notes.

TRIPLET. Three notes played in the time allocated for two; the basis for a swing or shuffle rhythm.

UNISON. A phrase played by more than one instrument at the same time.

VAMP. A short repeated melody or chord sequence.

WALKING BASS. A type of bassline where you play a different quarter-note on each beat to create a feeling of forward motion.

endnotes

[i] *Bass Player* January 1995

[ii] *Bass Player* January 2005

[iii] www.mikevisceglia.com/interviews.html

[1] Interview with Tony Bacon, November 30th 1994.

[2] Interview with Tony Bacon, November 30th 1994.

[3] Interview with Tony Bacon, November 30th 1994.

[4] *Beat Instrumental* October 1964.

[5] Interview with Spencer Leigh, 2000, BBC Radio Merseyside.

[6] Interview with Tony Bacon, November 30th 1994.

[7] *Beat Instrumental* October 1964.

[8] Interview with Tony Bacon, November 30th 1994.

[9] Interview with Tony Bacon, November 30th 1994.

[10] BBC Radio 2, September 2005.

[11] BBC Radio 2, December 1999.

[12] *Guitar Player* July 1990.

[13] *Melody Maker* August 21st & 28th 1971.

[14] *Melody Maker* August 21st & 28th 1971.

[15] Interview with Tony Bacon, November 30th 1994.

[16] Interview with Tony Bacon, November 30th 1994.

[17] *Beat Instrumental* October 1964.

[18] *Beat Instrumental* June 1965.

[19] Interview with Tony Bacon, November 30th 1994.

[20] Interview with Tony Bacon, November 30th 1994.

[21] *Beat Instrumental* June 1965.

[22] *Beat Instrumental* March 1964.

[23] MacDonald *Revolution In The Head*.

[24] *Chicago Tribune* February 12th 1964.

[25] *Beat Instrumental* October 1964.

[26] Interview with Tony Bacon, November 30th 1994.

[27] Interview with Tony Bacon, November 30th 1994.

[28] Interview with Tony Bacon, November 30th 1994.

[29] Interview with Tony Bacon, November 30th 1994.

[30] Interview with Tony Bacon, November 30th 1994.

[31] Interview with Tony Bacon, November 30th 1994.

[32] Interview with Tony Bacon, November 30th 1994.

[33] Interview with Tony Bacon, November 30th 1994.

[34] *Beat Instrumental* January 1966.

[35] Interview with Tony Bacon, November 30th 1994.

[36] Interview with Tony Bacon, November 30th 1994.

[37] Lewisohn *Complete Beatles Recording Sessions*.

[38] Massey *Behind The Glass*.

[39] Lewisohn *Complete Beatles Recording Sessions*.

[40] Droney *Mix Masters*.

[41] Simons *Analog Recording*.

[42] Interview with Ken Michaels www.totalaccesslive.com.

[43] Droney *Mix Masters*.

[44] Weinberg & Santelli *The Big Beat*.

[45] Interview with Tony Bacon, November 30th 1994.

[46] Miles *Paul McCartney*.

[47] Massey *Behind The Glass*.

[48] Droney *Mix Masters*.

[49] Miles *Paul McCartney*.

[50] Interview with Tony Bacon, November 30th 1994.

[51] Interview with Tony Bacon, November 30th 1994.

[52] Cunningham *Good Vibrations*.

[53] Interview with Ken Michaels www.totalaccesslive.com.

[54] Cunningham *Good Vibrations*.

[55] Lewisohn *Complete Beatles Recording Sessions*.

[56] Interview with Tony Bacon, November 30th 1994.

[57] *The Making Of Sgt Pepper* film, Really Useful/Walt Disney 1992.

[58] Interview with Tony Bacon, November 30th 1994.

[59] Babiuk *Beatles Gear*.

[60] *Beat Instrumental* November 1965.

[61] *Melody Maker* August 21st & 28th 1971.

[62] Interview with Tony Bacon, November 30th 1994.

[63] Martin & Pearson *With A Little Help From My Friends*.

[64] *Beat Instrumental* July 1967.

[65] Radio Luxembourg November 20th 1968.

[66] Interview with Tony Bacon, November 30th 1994.

[67] *Mix* January 2004.

[68] Interview with Tony Bacon, November 30th 1994.

[69] *The Beatles Anthology*, TV/video/DVD, 1995 etc.

[70] Interview with Tony Bacon, November 30th 1994.

[71] *Playboy* September 1980.

[72] Interview with Tony Bacon, November 30th 1994.

index

Song titles are in 'Single Quotes', album titles are *In Italics*.

acknowledgements

PHOTOGRAPHS

Here's a list to identify the sources for pictures in the book, with a bold-type locator or page number followed by the photographer / agency. **Jacket front** John Hopkins / Redfern's. **2** David Gray / Redfern's. **6** Jan Persson / Redfern's. **12** K&K Ulf Kruger / Redfern's. **20** K&K Ulf Kruger /Redfern's. **42** Cummings Archives / Redfern's. **62** David Magnus / Rex Features. **78** David Redfern / Redfern's.

BOOKS

This is a good place to note the debt that all Beatles students owe to Mark Lewisohn's research, brought together in his definitive books *The Complete Beatles Recording Sessions* and *The Complete Beatles Chronicle*. Another work of peerless research well worth spotlighting here is Andy Babiuk's equally definitive book on the group's equipment, *Beatles Gear*.

Andy Babiuk *Beatles Gear* Revised Edition (Backbeat 2002)
Mark Cunningham *Good Vibrations: A History Of Record Production* (Castle 1996)
Maureen Droney *Mix Masters: Platinum Engineers Reveal Their Secrets For Success* (Berklee Press 2003)
Pete Frame *The Beatles And Some Other Guys: Rock Family Trees Of The Early Sixties* (Omnibus 1997)
Guinness World Records *British Hit Singles & Albums* (Guinness 2005)
Bill Harry *The Beatles Encyclopedia* (Virgin 2000)
Mark Lewisohn *The Beatles Live!* (Pavilion 1986); *The Complete Beatles Chronicle* (Pyramid 1992); *The Complete Beatles Recording Sessions* (Hamlyn 1988)
Ian MacDonald *Revolution In The Head* (Pimlico 1995)
George Martin with William Pearson *With A Little Help From My Friends: The Making of Sgt. Pepper* (Little Brown 1994)
Barry Miles *Paul McCartney: Many Years From Now* (Vintage 1998)
Howard Massey *Behind The Glass* (Backbeat 2000)
David Simons *Analog Recording* (Backbeat 2006)
Max Weinberg with Robert Santelli *The Big Beat: Conversations With Rock's Great Drummers* (Contemporary 1984)

MAGAZINES AND PAPERS

We dug out (and really dug) material in back issues of the following publications during our research: *Beat Instrumental*; *The Chicago Tribune*; *Guitar Player*; *Melody Maker*; *Mix*; and *Playboy* (for the features, of course).

JACKET QUOTES

Lennon: *Playboy*, September 1980. Starr: Miles, *Paul McCartney*. Martin: Martin/Pearson *With A Little Help From My Friends*.

AUTHORS' THANKS

Tony Bacon would like to thank: Julie Bowie, Adrian Ashton, Chris Butler (Music Sales), Paul Cooper, Graham Gouldman, Dave Gregory, John Hammel, Sarah Holcroft (Music Sales), Russ Lease, Spencer Leigh, Mark Lewisohn, Barry Moorhouse, John Morrish, Greg Olwell (*Bass Player*), Jim Roberts, Dave Simons, Cat Walker (Music Sales), Shari Wied (Hal Leonard). Last and certainly not least, a very special nod to Paul McCartney for that generous, candid interview in 1994.

Gareth Morgan writes: I have one very personal and selfish reason for being so proud of my involvement in this book, and for enjoying it so much: my father, Trevor, who died on Christmas day, 1982, absolutely adored The Beatles even though they were way beyond the generation in which he grew up. He was 78 when he passed away, considerably older than my mother, so we're talking the 1920s as the decade when he would have been of the age to be listening to 'popular' music. Obviously the Charleston just didn't cut it for him. It gives me both a huge sense of contentment and achievement to think, with some justification, that he would have been really proud of this. This one's for you, dad. I would also like to thank Gwyn Mathias at Odessa studio, Andy Grant, Bob Gunter, Marcus Leadley, and John Callaghan at *Guitar & Bass* magazine, Theo Gordon, Steve Preston, Laurence Canty, Lynne Hoban, Brett Perry, Graham Stockley, John Bennett, Tony Ellis, Steve Salvari, Phil Overy, Jean and Owen Hooker, Tony Bacon for having faith in the first place, Eve Morgan (mum!), Lynne and Wayne Price, and especially Philippa for patience and support way beyond the call of duty.

MUSICAL SNIPPETS reproduced through the main text, in addition to the nine songs copyrighted in situ, are all copyright © Sony/ATV Songs LLC, copyright renewed, arrangements all copyright © 2006 Sony/ATV songs LLC, all rights administered by Sony/ATV Music Publishing, 8 Music Square West, Nashville, TN 37203, USA, international copyright secured, all rights reserved. We prepared a transcription and analysis of 'Something', our favourite piece of McCartney bass playing, but permission for us to reproduce this was declined by the licensor, Harrisongs. Sorry we couldn't share it with you.

"We forget. Who cares? We did some great stuff. But exact analysis was never our bag."
Paul McCartney on The Beatles' working methods